Starborn Books

Also by Paul Groves

ACADEME
MÉNAGE À TROIS
EROS AND THANATOS
WOWSERS
QWERTY

(All published by Seren)

Paul Groves

COUNTRY BOY

Starborn Books

COUNTRY BOY
Paul Groves

First published in 2007
by Starborn Books
Wales, U.K.

e-mail: sales@starbornbooks.co.uk
website: www.starbornbooks.co.uk

ISBN 978 1 899530 21 2

1

My father, Arthur Raymond Groves, was born on Sunday 8th September 1907. Henrik Ibsen had recently died in Christiania (not to be Oslo for another eighteen years), Pablo Picasso was busy renouncing perceptual art in favour of the conceptual kind, and New Zealand was becoming a dominion. Now he is dead it is his living self which is ghostly. His birthplace - 11 Stephens Court, Gloucester - has likewise become spectral. Nearby Westgate Street is naturally much changed from what he knew: boxy vehicles, canvas awnings, hatted men, short-trousered boys... He was the son of a waterman whose family plied their trade along the Severn. In 1928 he lived at 12 Priory Road, a byway which has largely disappeared. Betweentimes he had a basic education at Archdeacon School under the headmastership of Arthur Hawkins, then worked for G. Harris & Sons, Tailors, Hatters, Hosiers and Juvenile Outfitters, at 56 Southgate Street. In that year he sought employment with Birmingham City Police. Despite solid references from various worthies, he was informed in writing on 2nd October by Charles Haughton Rafter, their Chief Constable, that his attempt had been unsuccessful. Previously he had applied to join the Metropolitan force. When he tried his local constabulary he was accepted.

Over the next seventeen years he married, sired two children, and was stationed at Cirencester, at Coombe Hill on the A38, and at the riparian village of Twyning near Tewkesbury. During the war the conjugal knot unravelled. He subsequently courted a nurse, Mary Elisabeth Jenkins of Broxwood, Herefordshire. In 1946 she became pregnant and I was born the following year. In 1948 he and a fellow officer were involved in a brawl while arresting several inebriated louts in Gloucester city centre. This resulted in him receiving substantial injuries, early retirement, and an annual invalidity benefit of £300.11s.2d. For the sake of his health a move to the country was prescribed, hence the purchase of a bungalow near the Wye Valley in Monmouthshire. There was an irregular bus service and they had no car. My half-sister Janet attended Monmouth secondary modern school. My half-brother Douglas joined the Royal Navy.

I knew my father for twenty-six years. As he was four decades my senior it demanded something of an effort on his part to bridge the generation gap. Although this widened as I grew older, with time he mellowed and I became wiser so we reached an equable plateau.

In his youth he boxed and played rugby, sports which to me seemed incompatible with mental and dental health. My recollections are of someone not averse to gardening and occasional carpentry, but otherwise happy to fill an armchair with his blossoming girth. He rose early, reflecting a regime of many years' shift work, and was rarely late to bed. He snored like a dragon. Mother was a cowed St. George, dreaming of sleep and praying for oblivion. I encountered such tortuous proximity only once. He was thinking of buying a village shop and had arranged a train journey to Lampeter in Cardiganshire. From the station a taxi took us into a darkness which even its headlights failed properly to penetrate. It was denser than fog: a moonless, starless night in the wilds, the lanes silent, the wider world invisible. Finally we arrived at an outpost of civilisation: Llwyn-y-groes, on the Llangeitho road. Wind moaned around stout walls. A fire glowed within. Faces were from another century, tongues from a far country. We talked by a slow-ticking clock in the parlour till I dropped off against his arm. Eventually he roused me and we clambered upstairs. He prepared for slumber and followed me to downy pillows and caressing sheets. The mattress sank, and I drowsily rolled, frowning, towards him. There was not much to me. He more than made up for my slim twelve years. I shrugged and resumed my rest. Then it started. For eight hours I craved the repose he enjoyed. I murmured, fidgeted, stuffed fingers in ears, dunked my head under the blankets. There was no respite, only rhythmic roughness rubbing the air, rattling on, on, on. Next morning he bounced downstairs to consume a hearty breakfast. I looked as if I had attended a wake. I vowed never again to attempt to sleep with my father.

After fifty he grew corpulent. Our village was surrounded by woods he chose not to walk in. Mother and I wandered for miles accompanied by our dog. Dad stayed at home, pottering, filling out pools coupons, studying racing form, reading the Bible... not fiction, poetry, or biography. He was interested solely in gaining something tangible from his labours; that would hardly have included his exact contemporary W.H. Auden, even if he had heard of him. He occasionally wrote Victorian drivel of the a-little-walk-with-Jesus variety. It was as sentimental as a calendar illustrated with kittens and violets. This, I suppose, encapsulated his ideal aesthetic. He was not blessed or cursed with my ironical appreciations, my acquired cynicism. He was big-hearted or silly enough in later years to stop the car he had by then and offer a gang of council workmen a boiled sweet each. To the best of my knowledge none ever told him to frig off. Some even said 'Sir' when thanking him.

He was irascible, prone to childish outbursts, yet essentially a softie who would melt if a steeplechaser broke its leg. During my teenage years his hero was not John F. Kennedy or Nikita Khrushchev but Terry Biddlecombe, the National Hunt jockey with the engaging grin. When *Nijinsky* won the 1970 Triple Crown - the 2000 Guineas, Derby, and St. Leger - I am sure he had no idea the mount was named after a Russian dancer.

About some things he had an obscurantist ignorance. He told me once, in all seriousness, the moon emitted rather than reflected light. Likewise, he would not proceed with the rules of chess when he realised only knights could jump. This he considered unfair. I never progressed to explaining why rooks did not have beaks and why two are white. Draughts seemed altogether more egalitarian and less needlessly complex. He taught me cribbage, using worn cards and spent matches, but no outdoor pursuits. Nonetheless I remain grateful for his presence if not his tutelage. When it came to homework he was hardly the fount of wisdom I would have had him be. Mother was little better. Neither knew any Latin or Greek, and his linguism in matters Gallic extended no further than *Cherchez la femme*, scant use when wanting your puncture fixed in Provence. Thus astronomy and languages were out so far as assistance was concerned, as was his smattering of jurisprudence. Mother's medical training was of no assistance either. Our only historical textbook was Charles Dickens's *A Child's History of England* which this child found indigestible. He hardly considered himself chronologically illiterate though. He knew 1066 to be the year of the you-know-what and this was sufficient. In his own eyes he was a rounded man, in others' eyes increasingly a round one. Had the Open University started in, say, 1949 rather than 1969 he would still not have availed himself of its services. He never went abroad other than on a day trip to Ostend. He ventured no further north than Blackpool, nor did he ever enter an aeroplane or a submarine. His world went on two wheels, then four, or on shank's pony. He met the Aga Khan and the future Edward VIII yet had not a fraction of their cosmopolitan ease. He was a victim of his limited experiences. The lives of the great and the good from Pharaoh Hor-Aha to Sir Stafford Cripps largely escaped him. However, he was the only father I will ever have and he could have been ten times worse.

My parents were baptised as Seventh Day Adventists, lapsing after a few years. During this time we were taken to Sabbath services in Hereford by our pastor, Arthur Lacey, a gregarious bachelor who maniacally drove a Hillman Minx. Sibling schoolmates Michael and Marilyn Reynolds sometimes accompanied us, six filling a car meant for four. The worshippers convened in, appropriately, an upper room, which was to religiosity what Dorothy Parker was to reticence. The venue was a nondescript red-brick building off Edgar Street. The stairs creaked, and the chairs might have excited the German designer Walter Gropius with their tubular-steel functionalism but did little for me. As a nod towards mainstream Christianity there was a simple cross on a table, and our hymns were indistinguishable from other Nonconformist groups'. Dad occasionally preached. When it came to the sermon, or 'address' as it was usually called, anything went, depending on the speaker's bias. I did not object to all this per se, though would have far preferred spending time with a bird-watcher's manual. These turgid renditions of fundamentalist zeal left me cold. The congregation consisted of a dozen or so widows and spinsters and the type of old boy who might buttonhole you at a bus stop. They - we - presumably needed an emotional crutch. We were lonely, failed, and impoverished, and craved in the next world what was denied us in this.

My parents' initiation had been by total immersion. Instead of being ducked in the dubious waters of an Arkansas creek, they took on the liquid mantle of salvation at an indoor baptistry reached by the lifting of a large trapdoor. While they and others filed seraphically towards their moment of reckoning, a choir hummed like a UFO on cruise control. Floral headiness enveloped us. The minister nasally pontificated, flanked by two po-faced heavies. These robots sprang to life with each candidate, several of whom briefly resisted as they went under. It was like a scene from *A Clockwork Orange* only infinitely nicer. Mother wafted towards me smiling and dripping, heedless of her ruined perm. Had the singers been on vinyl they would have finished by now. These prefigured the age of auto-reverse audio cassette and kept going. This happened in Newport, South Wales rather than Hereford. The time of true oneness arrived when we trekked to S.D.A. headquarters at Stanborough Park, Watford. It was to be my introduction to the sights of London. I was eleven. The week consisted almost entirely of pious meetings. It was unrelievedly stodgy, reflecting the mood of postwar Britain. No wonder Cliff Richard's first single, released that year, was called *Move It*.

Dad did more than attend odd assemblages on a Saturday. He went door to door selling religious tracts and attempting to convert the natives. Whether he achieved any such transformations is unclear, though his homely techniques of persuasion certainly sold enough material. House by house, street by street, he tramped the Forest of Dean area peddling thousands of goodly treatises. While preparing breakfast or shaving he would sing the likes of *Night and Day* and *Begin the Beguine*. I did not understand how this qualified him to be known as Cole Porter. It was some time before I realised he was a colporteur, something else entirely. Once he had done his stint for the Lord he decided to turn his efforts in another direction and started flogging houses. He installed a phone and worked from home, undercutting competitors and giving a personal service. It paid off.

Had he lived into old age he might have retired somewhere swish like Torquay where in a desirable clifftop residence we could have overlooked Thatcher Rock and mused upon the rewards of private enterprise. It was not to be. In 1972 he was smitten by the collywobbles. Nothing serious, just a slight ache. As dyspepsia was unofficially diagnosed, camomile tea was prescribed. I said he needed exercise. He shrugged, and reduced his sugar intake. This in no way interfered with his alcohol consumption. Although I never saw him drunk, I often found him not entirely sober. He rarely indulged at home. Mostly drink was a passport to convivial socialising. The ache continued. He reluctantly sought medical advice, which transposed into medical attention at Hereford County Hospital, which in turn prompted a surgeon's summons. We met in the ward sister's office: mother, my young wife, myself, and a harassed specialist with too many pens in his breast pocket, a flop of hair across his forehead, and the manner of a distracted don.

"I'm afraid I have some deeply unsettling news for

you." We looked at each other and back at the consultant.

Who should speak next? I took it upon myself to do so. "How bad is it?"

He considered. "Not good at all."

The next question almost asked itself. "Is he going to get better?"

He looked up, fixing me with soft grey eyes. "There's nothing we can do." Mother caught her breath. My wife held her arm, as if expecting her to stand and accost the physician. "Cancer of the stomach. Radiotherapy and chemotherapy would be useless. They might have helped had we seen him earlier. Now it's out of control."

"How long does he have?"

We were told it would be two months at the most and probably quite a bit less.

He was transferred to Monmouth Cottage Hospital, looking as right as rain. Acid rain. The kind that would eat into the surface of our lives. He tired easily. We did not tell him. Somehow he knew. Letters were dictated, putting his affairs in order. My parents had moved from The Narth, the village where they had spent nearly a quarter of a century, the previous year. Everything was under control. During the last days mother nursed him at home. He slept like a baby, face increasingly sallow, all humour gone as if it had been banished by a new type of reality. I spent hours at the bed-side: wearisome, of course, but I could not think of anywhere better. The life ebbed out of him at 11.00 a.m. on Wednesday 21st November 1973 - St. Cecilia's Eve. W.H. Auden had died less than two months earlier, also aged sixty-six. His last poem, a haiku, could as easily have applied to my father:

> He still loves life
> But O O O O how he wishes
> The good Lord would take him.

The cremation took place at Gloucester. He had come full

circle. It had been decided to scatter the ashes beside his parents' grave in the cemetery off Tredworth Road. The service was adequate. We had to wait our turn as loved ones we had never met bemoaned another's passing. Afterwards we had to look sharp as further distraught relatives were queueing. Mafiosi-style undertakers stood near large black cars impatiently sucking the life from cigarettes which they would finally discard with a measure of disgust beside the rhododendrons. It was all very subdued, a matter of looking downcast for a reasonable period. Minimally dignified. There was no jostling. The chimney had shades of Dachau. Years later I nailed the experience in a poem subsequently published in *Literary Review*.

Twenty Minutes

We entered as another group were leaving.
Our black coats made us Russian politicians,
Sombre and snowbound; yet around us visions
Of summer blossomed. Everything was living.
We took our seats. The place did not feel sinister,
Merely sad. Untold scenes of grief
Had permeated everything. "His life
Should make us glad we knew him," said the minister
Chestily. A cheerless tape clicked on.
The curtains parted like the Red Sea waters
Then joined again. Our father disappears
A million times towards the waiting oven.
We walked back to the cars and no one spoke.
The August sky had one thin skein of smoke.

Here the season has changed from autumn to summer. Poetic licence, calculated to contrast the lifelessness within with the liveliness without. The rest is approximately correct. What it does not state is that five of us drove to the nearest steakhouse and had a slap-up meal, covering ourselves with the proviso

'It's what he would have wanted'. For the first time since about 1910 there was no way of confirming this. After a lustrum, mother gave his clothes to a jumble sale, burned their love letters, and passed on a few effects to me. For years afterwards I could see some of his hairs in a brush when I visited her home; his stick of shaving cream remained in the bathroom cabinet; evidence of his handwriting was in a dozen places. Did he have a good life? It could have been better: dancing at the Savoy, motoring down to Antibes in a Bugatti, viewing the midnight sun from Tromsö while sipping cloudberry liqueur. He was somewhat bigoted and chauvinistic yet seamed with kindness and overall on the side of the angels. I am proud to have been his son.

2

My mother was born on Thursday 18th September 1919 and came from a lost world. Not Sir Arthur Conan Doyle's deserted island where, on a scientific trip, intrepid explorers encountered prehistoric animals, but a corner of a quiet English county, a region which still manages to evoke yesteryear despite being no longer quite the overlooked area she knew. Her birthplace was Sunny Bank, a house just off the A480 Woonton-to-Lyonshall road, and she was brought up at a cottage called Bonds Green less than a mile to the north-east across fields and the Broxwood Court estate. Above arched the silent Herefordshire sky and in every direction a country peace extended, a slumbrous calm which remains to some extent discernible by the visitor. The nearest town was Kington, where she attended Lady Hawkins' Grammar School. Beyond, the Welsh hills start. Immediately you encounter Hergest Ridge, memorialised by musician

Mike Oldfield in his 1974 album of that name. Even nearer to her roots lay the village of Almeley, whence hailed Sir John Oldcastle, model for Shakespeare's Sir John Falstaff.

My maternal grandmother Amy Hoby was of a Radnorshire family which rose to prominence in Tudor times. According to an 1888 Harleian Society publication, their lineage is traceable to Rhys Gryg, Prince of Deheubarth, who died in 1234. William Hoby of Leominster had four sons, the eldest of whom - Philip - was employed by Henry VIII in diplomatic service at the Spanish and Portuguese courts and was a friend of Titian. The Manor of Bisham in Berkshire was bestowed upon him. Bisham Abbey, which he built, is where Elizabeth I was held captive from 1555 to 1558 and where Warwick the Kingmaker lies buried. To this day its east wing is haunted by Sir Philip's wife, an eminent scholar and close friend of the queen.

My mother did not boast about her noble antecedents. By the time she was born the First World War had ended and her father Edward had returned from Dartmoor prison after incarceration as a conscientious objector. He was a Quaker and a pacifist, as was Amy. They occupy adjacent plots in the Friends' Meeting-House graveyard at Almeley Wootton. Mary was their firstborn. Next came Fred, Edward, Ivy, Elsie, and Ruth. Quietude and privacy must have been virtually non-existent in their household.

After eighteen months living at 10 Hemmylock Road, Selly Oak and travelling by tram to the Dorothy Gosling Secretarial College in Corporation Street, Birmingham, she changed direction to become a nurse. Her sister Ivy trained to be one too, and at Luton and Dunstable Hospital attended George Bernard Shaw during his final illness. My mother did stints at Hereford, Bromsgrove, Tewkesbury, and Gloucester - all by the age of twenty-eight, when she hung up her fob-watch, discarded her starched cap and precise uniform, and took to wifehood and motherhood full time. My father would brag in later years that she had risen high in the profession: boloney - she attained the rank of sister and that was that. Small brown-and-white photographs show her posing in sunlight with assorted TB patients during the forties. Throughout my childhood I fondly imagined she somehow embodied the spirit of therapeutic care, a latter-day Florence Nightingale labouring selflessly among the wards and corridors of an English Scutari. Faintly glamorous, certainly idealistic, but wide of the mark.

While at Sunnyside, my first home at The Narth, she provided bed and breakfast for ramblers from, predominantly, the Midlands, the West Country, and South Wales, yet was dissuaded from continuing as my father claimed she was undercharging and overgenerous. Perhaps she regarded them as healthy patients to whom she needed to minister. Thereafter, at a bungalow we had built and named Shangri La, we started a shop - first in the kitchen, next in a garden shed. The post office was the village's main retail outlet; nonetheless, we did a respectable trade. This and running the home absorbed her energies and increased her contacts. Simply to attend to her husband and child would have proved isolative.

Later she learned to drive. My portly father would be chauffeured by her hither and thither. He was not the balmiest companion and initially was overprotective and prescriptive, rather in the manner of a rally navigator: 'Watch that child!' 'Careful on the bend!' 'Use your indicator!' Sometimes he would provoke exasperation, prompting her to stop and refuse to restart until he shut his trap. Chastened, he would do so for a mile or so. When they began their estate agency they seemed to be out every day and most evenings. I was at college and saw little of them. Their years of having to depend upon slow and infrequent public transport were over.

Our last vacation was in the late sixties. We and Joy Wood, my then girlfriend, drove down to Christchurch, Hampshire for a week in a caravan. Decades earlier he had taken Douglas, Janet, and his first wife (also named Mary) to nearby Mudeford. The jaunt was partly to relive old memories. My parents rarely holidayed. A long weekend at Weston-super-Mare or a few days enjoying the proletarian delights of Butlin's, Minehead more or less summed up their travels during this period. Their first break had been to war-ravaged Swansea in 1946. They lodged at The Mumbles and explored nearby coves and beaches. The following poem recounts their excursion to one in particular.

A Bay on the Gower Peninsula

A monochrome snap proves
that on July 23rd 1946 my parents
visited Pwll Du. Its waves
welcomed their unheralded presence,

and they stayed, perhaps all afternoon.
They never told me about that foray,
and not until they had gone
did I discover this trapped memory,

less than a second's exposure to draw
me back half a century later,
wondering which track they took, how
they behaved, what the weather

was like (the photograph does not
reliably convey such data, but points
solely to this inaccessible spot).
Long decades since

have taken too much:
only in this youthful representation
are the years absent. Then the beach
was immediate, smooth stone

seemingly as recent as new bread.
I was yet to be conceived, merely a blur
of possibility in either head;
and the future promised to last forever.

Their expectancy is my history.
I know how their dreams turned out:
unexceptional, part of the human story,
easily forgettable, not worth writing about -

yet write I will, for they were bold
in their love and idealism in those days
and the world refused to wither and grow old
and the sun was full of praise.

After my father's death, my mother - by now settled in Wyesham, a Monmouth suburb - threw herself into good works: Red Cross, Women's Guild, Methodist Fellowship, hospital visiting... and developed a circle of friends. My wife and I visited frequently from our Forest of Dean home. She lived to see both granddaughters arrive and evolve into schoolgirls. Despite bouts of diverticulitis, the tiresome presence of osteoporosis, and arthritis which reduced her hands to the gnarled appearance of old tree roots, she maintained her curiosity about life, her religious conviction, and her sense of humour. When she died on All Saints' Day 1996 a good many grieved. Our family might not have been extensive but supportive neighbours and associates more than compensated. She expired during the small hours of Friday 1st November in a side ward of Nevill Hall Hospital, Abergavenny, the official cause bronchopneumonia and intestinal obstruction. My wife and I saw her for the final time the previous afternoon. She was wearing a nebulizer, a mask through which a sedative was being administered. Fluid retention had distended her abdomen; her breaths were rapid and slight. I said the Lord's Prayer beside her bed. Her lips moved with the words, and she managed an 'Amen'. Before we left, heavy with tears and the almost-certain realisation we would never see her alive again, she turned, half opened her eyes, and croaked a few words. I drew near and asked for a repeat. These were, after all, the last I would hear her utter. Would they be valedictory sentiments, a strained farewell, a whispered hope? No. They were commonplace and oddly cheering. She was looking to the future as ever, anticipatory and alive. She wanted to know what had come in the morning's mail. "Any post?" she enquired with genuine interest. "No," I said, "I don't believe there is." Before leaving I said "I love you". Then I closed the door.

3

Although a presiding influence during my childhood was the conifer, in various shapes and sizes, the forests in which they grew were not exclusively green. They were cathedrals of brown and purple, cool shadowy realms which sunlight penetrated obliquely. There were grey squirrels and foxes but no deer. There were broad buckler ferns, wood sorrel, and brambles. In season the needle litter would be punctuated by pine-wood mushrooms. Underfoot the *Formica rufa* or wood ant laboured ceaselessly. These inspiring insects made hills as big as dustbins and as complex as transistors, except that transistors were invented in the year of my birth whereas wood ants have been toiling since time immemorial.

Our first home was of timber. Black-and-white snapshots show me always out-of-doors, probably because my parents' primitive camera lacked a flashlight and exposure meter. Consequently the reinforced memory is of bright unbuttoned days. The narrow roads were nearly as non-vehicular as the nineteenth century. Delivery vans chugged from Trellech with groceries, and now and then you would see an ancient taxi wobble round the bend like something off a carousel. Generally the wind bore only birdsong or voices. It felt as bypassed as the gentle rural Sweden of Arne Sucksdorff's *The Great Adventure* of 1953, a film no aspirant cineaste should miss. Days passed quietly, enlivened by nothing more exciting than my assaults on the chicken run with a switch. The birds would leap, squawking, into the air like Disney characters, crashing into each other and landing in a dustcloud. This was good free entertainment. We must have had the lithest poultry for miles.

My first memory is of Janet, a shy buxom teenager, pushing me in the pram to a house called The Pleck where Mrs. Roberts sold paraffin. We passed the school, a snug bastion of stone and slate, and the post office, residence of the redoubtable Nellie Harris. Few aeroplanes were ever seen. No television aerials challenged the skyline. Mains drainage did not exist. Well water predominated. Clothes were plain or downright dowdy; there was little reason for them not to be. Everyone you passed gave a greeting, something I still miss. Most stopped to chat - not sitcomspeak spiked with innuendo, but unobtrusive bucolic tittle-tattle. There was hardly any scandal. The gossip was of a general nature: *Have you seen so-and-so lately?* or *How's whatshisname?* I knew of no crime committed during my years there, and no drunkenness (the nearest public house was a two-mile walk away). In the evenings people listened to the wireless, read, knitted, played cards, or simply talked.

If this sounds idyllic, it was. If it sounds as straitly pure in heart as the Plymouth Colony of the Pilgrim Fathers, it was not. There was no religious observance in the village apart from at the school. If you wanted to follow Psalm 98 and make a joyful noise unto the Lord you would either do so in the bathtub or visit Maryland. Although its name suggests booking a flight to Baltimore, in reality you would need go no further than the next settlement - a scattering of dwellings a mile hence through the trees. Any woman could walk in the woods unmolested and fearless. Mothers and toddlers went to the Bethel weekly; grandparents joined them; some fathers attended. The hymns were lustily delivered. The collection plate resembled a metal hill on a baize plain when brought to the altar for blessing. Christmas parties in the annexe were among the best fun I have ever had. Although anniversaries were nerve-racking, nobody coshed you if you got it wrong. Once a year we stood hesitantly in front of a sea of hats, perfume, tightly knotted ties, and brilliantined hair, and declaimed stanzas penned a hundred years earlier.

If Wesleyanism was not your preference you could always slope off to Whitebrook Baptist Chapel, 'slope' being the operative word, for Whitebrook occupied a steep-sided valley which met the River Wye near the elegant 160-foot span of Bigsweir Bridge. My poem 'The Anniversaries' evokes those days and that atmosphere and first appeared in *The Anglo-Welsh Review*.

> All are dead, the old ladies
> who used to beam reassuringly
> at our unease. They had always
> been that age, like the sea,
> enthusiasm in waves
> up the chapel aisle. Christ saves
>
> boys from drowning in tweeness,
> I'd hoped. Little white collar,
> polished black shoes, a heinous
> Brylcreem shine: you stood there
> reciting pious doggerel
> which usually went down well.
>
> An awesomely perfect girl
> - flouncy ribbons and bows,

a lacy unreal whirl
of confection, retroussé nose,
clean knickers - would stand up next.
We were angelic unsexed

dwarves. A royal court
would have loved us. Some Spanish king
would have given us sweetmeats, bought
tutors, and everything
would have been lutes and oysters
and darkling Moorish cloisters.

But this was fifties Wales
in a valley few had heard of.
The walls were mosses, snails
and dampness. No word of
progress might filter through
ever. Nothing seemed new:

life was tinged with the eerie.
We were askance and wary....
All that has gone for ever
yet no beauty, pain, or rage,
nothing grown-up or clever,
can rival that makeshift stage.

If I owe my early poetic development to anyone other than
my mother, who plied me with nursery rhymes and *The Song
of Hiawatha* during toddlerhood, it is to Dwight and Ira, those
stirring revivalists who, under their surnames Moody and
Sankey, gave us *Sacred Songs and Solos* in 1873. I have been
wooed by the likes of J.M. Neale since, in *Hymns Ancient &
Modern*, but it is to the former influence that I am tempted to
return.

Sunday School filled us equally with hope and dread.
Angels resembled our chickens - lots of white feathers,

though with shining androgynous faces. The apocalyptic creatures of Revelation 4 never ceased to sing *Holy, holy, holy*. I had a sneaking suspicion even God would tire of this after a while. As ours is the age of the debunker (devil's advocacy *de rigueur*, the word 'doubt' commonly prefixed by the word 'healthy') the single-minded, simple-minded vision of the Bible as presented then almost seems attractive.

Primary school was bliss. We were never snowed under by a plethora of multicoloured learning aids; there were not hundreds in assembly; and we were not allowed to argue with the teacher. If he was wrong we endured it with a stiff upper lip. Nobody made us sit in chatty little groups. If we did not pull our socks up they were forcibly pulled up for us. Despite the mental demands of mathematics, we arrived at our eleventh year numerate. Three miles away at Cleddon Hall on Saturday 18th May 1872 the philosopher Bertrand Russell had been born. In his autobiography he wrote:

> *At the age of eleven, I began Euclid, with my brother as my tutor. This was one of the great events of my life, as dazzling as first love. I had not imagined that there was anything so delicious in the world. After I had learned the fifth proposition, my brother told me that it was generally considered difficult, but I had found no difficulty whatever. This was the first time it had dawned upon me that I might have some intelligence.*

School had two classes: the Little Room for infants, the Big Room for juniors. Miss James was our first teacher, Mr. Vernal our last. They oversaw all learning from five to eleven, and provided a strict grounding in the three Rs: Riting, Rithmetic, and Reading, so called because had they been known by their true initials this would have spelt WAR, the last thing wanted in classrooms. After lunch, which I ate at home, we messed around with paints, crayons, and raffia, or went on splendid nature walks, a happy band of pilgrims following our very own Gladys Aylward. We searched in summery hedgerows for hart's-tongue ferns, dog roses, common violets, and lesser celandines; we pondered the ways of mouse and chaffinch, butterfly and hedgehog. None of us had yet seen a *Coca-Cola* can idly discarded on a verge, international symbol of the throwaway society; and although Hiroshima had been atomised a mere decade earlier we had not been told about it. We were more aware of Sir Walter Scott's *Quentin Durward* than of President Dwight D. Eisenhower. From the lanes we tumbled into the woods. The harsh call of a jay echoed around us. We gambolled in leaf litter and were roundly scolded for pelting each other with the stuff. "Find me a wood anemone," charged Miss James, "but don't pick it." We raced off, only partly consumed by our quest. Cuckoo-pint, white helleborine, and bird's-nest orchids were identified. Above us *Fagus sylvatica*, the magisterial beech, towered.

Wordsworth's assertion 'Heaven lies about us in our infancy' is too pat. Try saying it to a scrawny bundle sucking emaciated paps in the Sahel, its face festooned with flies. However, it *can* be true. We had no steady income, car, electricity, or holidays, yet I felt princely rather than deprived. Food sprang miraculously from the earth; mother represented an endless fount of love and understanding; child abuse was unheard-of, as was any form of counselling - appropriate or otherwise. One could run in any direction under the sky's vast dome, fearing nothing worse than scabby knees. From intimidating the hens and dropping my father's carpentry tools down the well at Sunnyside, I had entered both Miss James's stern gaze and a new bungalow named after the wondrous Himalayan kingdom in James Hilton's 1933 best-seller *Lost Horizon*. The name is now as twee as Dunroamin or Honeysuckle Cottage. Then, it was not. Compared with the Anglo-Americanism of current society where families are drip-fed on television and few sports are unblemished by advertising, The Narth had some claim to being thought paradisiacal.

My closest friends - Rosemary Allin, Allan Bidmead,

David Brinkman, Reuben Kedward, Lyndon Morris, and Marilyn Reynolds - were a well-adjusted bunch. Their parents had not divorced and their upbringing was balanced. The boys wore shorts, except in winter, and the girls wore skirts. The worst words we ever heard were 'bloody' and 'bugger'. As for taboo Saxonisms, they were not encountered until much later.

And so we played after school until dusk, when curtains were drawn and Tilley lamps lit. I sketched and coloured at the large oak table while mum knitted and dad did magazine competitions (especially the obscure *Bullets*) or dozed, lulled by the wireless. My mongrel companion for a decade was Nigger, a creature whose name raised no eyebrows. He would be curled up on the hearth rug, and the universe would be reduced to the confines of the living room, whose lighting resembled that found in the classicist paintings of Georges de La Tour. Rarely did I go to bed later than nine. The dog had a basket in the kitchen, and my parents slept in the only other bedroom.

Little lads in Acapulco probably itch to follow tradition in a hurtling descent towards the waves. I ached instead to ascend via any branches which would support me. Forget shade and lumber: trees were incontrovertibly for climbing. What could be nicer than to scale a cross between an alp and a central nervous system? Armed only with crampons of enthusiasm, I would shin up the nearest sycamore in a trice. This was all very well until the fateful day I lost my nerve. Suddenly derring-do deserted me. I shouted repeatedly for help. A Pakistani itinerant was at our back door, turbaned, suited, with one case of undergarments and another of cheap ties. He halted in mid-sentence, Peter Sellers impersonating a stereotypical colonial.

"Madam, I think I am hearing something. Maybe it comes from over there." He pointed towards a tall dense hedge.

"You're right," exclaimed my mother, brushing past him. She ran to the base of where the disembodied cries came from. "I'm coming," she called. What happened next is de-

28

scribed in a poem published in the Canadian journal *Wascana Review*:

Climbing Trees

There was little point
to the escapade.
> *Perhaps it aped*
growing up, lording it over adults
reduced to ticktack specialists
mouthing imprecations about
cancelled supper.
> *Sycamores*
were best. They supported
with dependable arms, and hid you
with leaves as big as lily pads.
You could part branches, and watch
the horizon unroll like a tradesman's carpet,
see into others' gardens, espy
lawnmower battleships, the cannonry
of red-hot pokers, the geometric lakes
of winking greenhouses.
> *You could*
change a dog to an ant, launch
spittle majestically, and rediscover
the New World like Amerigo Vespucci.
There was spice to the meal: the promise
of paralysis, the threat posed
by a wrong move.
> *Once*
mother had to mount a rescue attempt,
a stalwart descent to blocked passageways
and trapped potholers, only in reverse,
her rising face a helium-filled
balloon of hope.
> *I remember how we fell*

together through that green gauntlet,
the earth rushing to meet us like an angry relative.

Cuts and bruises. Father apoplectic. "You could have *killed* her...." The salesman backing off from the door, unwilling to become embroiled in a domestic drama. Next time, I steeled myself against an egress of courage and everything returned to normal. My perch that of a thrush demarcating its territory, I trilled across the village. Lyndon Morris responded in kind. His mother often came out to summon their dog; her *Jerry!* almost matched my warble in intensity. Lyndon's father, Vernon, gave haircuts in his garage for a few pence. Across the road John and Tony Jones's mother Brenda greeted you with a smile. What uncomplicated lives everyone led! How lacking in rancour. There was hardly any more stressful activity than taking the top off a milk bottle. With enough of these shiny gold or silver circles you could turn a scarecrow into a pearly king or queen. Theoretically, birds should have fled in terror when confronted by this unnatural glitter. In practice they found it rather fetching, a pleasant distraction while ripping through a row of peas.

Beyond Brenda's garden lay a special field. It was not much more than half an acre yet once a year it lit up the entire county. Until the end of October it would not have merited a second glance. Then it started gaining old tyres, a spent mattress, off-cuts of wood, cardboard boxes, anything combustible heaped in an unholy fashion until one was left in no doubt that a delicious barbaric ritual was in the offing. It became complete when topped by a stuffed mannequin. I am sure no one understood what was to be celebrated. Were we really raising a hurrah because a hapless explosives expert, newly recruited in Flanders, had been caught guarding thirty-six barrels in a Westminster cellar? Were we to whoop and whirl because Robert Catesby, the plot's originator, died - besieged by the Sheriff of Worcester - in a pool of blood, a picture of the Blessed Virgin pressed to his lips? The commemoration, which has nothing to do with blighting Catholicism, remains a travesty and a farce, but how enjoyable it was! From the lounge bay window I watched for hours, fearful they might start without me. We never got there early enough. The pyre was always lit before mother and I arrived. *Whoosh. Bang.* The words sound flat and hackneyed: the experience never was. People became moving orange masks and busy fingers, pointillist spectres seen through a sparky haze, grinning pagans intent on banishing the dark. More resurrection than death, it could have celebrated the winter solstice.

Carol singing was another sacred rite. An absence of streetlights rendered the village inky at night. A torch was all that lay between you and deadly precipices. Although there were not any, it felt as if there were. Wide dark skies and silent lanes fostered in one a brooding melancholy. It was no surprise a certain Miss Rossetti came to mind. None of your Slade belting out the raucous perennial *Merry Christmas Everybody*. More apposite was the tenor of Christina's contribution:

> In the bleak mid-winter
> > Frosty wind made moan;
> Earth stood hard as iron,
> > Water like a stone.
> Snow had fallen, snow on snow,
> > Snow on snow,
> In the bleak mid-winter
> > Long ago.

Nothing there about religion. It is a retrospective report from the London Weather Centre. Nonetheless, it held me in thrall, as did Gustav Holst's setting of it. Certain other tunes were equally haunting: *I saw three ships come sailing in* had undeniable freshness, while the Czech carol *Little Jesus, sweetly sleep* was similarly beguiling. I trudged around the village, pockets at the ready for whatever largesse might materialise. At May Cottages Mrs. Light once bellowed down the hall 'Come back nearer Christmas!'. Although she had a point, I never returned. Organised forays were rare, as the nearest church was at Trellech. Mostly it was left to greedy boys to harass householders with indifferently sung ditties until bribed to go away. How satisfying to hammer on doors, fuelled by the spirit of entrepreneurship, and intone those lyrics. The delightful upshot was umpteen threepenny bits and sixpences. Heavy pennies and halfpennies were accepted grudgingly.

With yuletide safely past, the long haul to Easter began, during which the weather would turn ugly. Kerosene heaters in the hall warded off hypothermia. I occasionally slept fully clothed. Icicles multiplied. North-westerlies fashioned snow-drifts as high as window ledges. Everyone did a silly walk, a step forward and one sideways, or else slid backwards, or fell over. Robins flapped from relinquished Christmas cards into the real world, looking distinctly non-festive. Crows provided stark contrast to a white wilderness as they winged across the breadth of another joyless minute. The nineteen fifties were melting slowly. Janet went nursing and married. Douglas joined the police force like his father. When the buds appeared I climbed more trees. When summer came the field beside our home was scythed. Mother raked the hay. To the north lay Colonel's Park, to the south Manor Wood, to the west Beacon Hill, and to the east the unseen Wye, snaking to the Severn Estuary a dozen miles away. Beyond its valley reared the hills of Dean and a castle which had never seen a battle: that of St Briavels, in King John's reign a hunting lodge. Near it St. Mary's church raised an admonitory Norman finger through-out my childhood, pointing to the need for less worldly con-cerns and standing as a reminder that England was technically my fatherland, not wild Wales. Be that as it may, it is to The Narth that thoughts home like racing pigeons. Australian Abo-rigines have their alcheringa, a mythical golden age they visit in dreams: mine extends from 1950 to 1960 and occupies a leafy redoubt high among the east Gwent hills. Five miles distant, less than two centuries before, Wordsworth had composed his famous lines above Tintern Abbey. His sentiments prefigured mine exactly. *That time is past, And all its aching joys are now no more, And all its dizzy raptures.*

Mr. Vernal was keen for us to sit some examination or other and urged us to reach a good standard in Arithmetic and English. Several of us diligently tried. The ordeal arrived. The eleven-plus. Of course! This was the ogre reputed to feed on the bodies of Less Able Children. I kept danger at bay by working neatly and quickly and double-checking everything. It was felt there were only two scholarship candidates that summer: myself and Rosemary. During those long warm days we shared a bond which was rather touching. Suddenly, after knowing each other for six years, we became close. Our amity evaporated as unaccountably as it had arrived when the results appeared. Only one of us had passed this dreadful test. She would be committed to the everlasting darkness of a secondary modern school while I would saunter through the ringing cloisters of a Headmasters' Conference School - yet she was every bit as clever as I was supposed to be. In July Mr. Vernal awarded me a book 'for the most consistent work' of the academic year. Had he discerned my interest in birds? Or was this to be a rattling good yarn in the spirit of R.M. Ballantyne? I raced home and breathlessly discarded the wrapper in front of delighted parents. My heart sank. It might as well have been *Basque for Beginners* or *The Althing: A History of the Icelandic Parliament.* To this day I have not fathomed why he gave me a primer on cacti propagation.

The week beginning Monday 22nd September 1958 saw a scrubbed willowy lad awaiting the school bus at the foot of our lane. It was 8.20 a.m. and I creaked with newness. Stiff new leather satchel, stiff new leather shoes, stiff new cap, stiff new blazer and trousers. I had almost to be lifted like a cardboard cutout onto the throbbing vehicle. Mike

Reynolds, who had passed the eleven-plus the previous year, would show me the ropes. I felt sick with excitement. Here and there were other minuscule meritocrats, some female. Did any know what algebra was, or if Moody and Sankey hymns were sung in Chapel? Could someone quickly state the rules of rugby? Scrums, rucks, and dead balls sounded serious - especially dead balls. And what of the classics? And prep? And.... No one was about to let on.

4

Over the thirteenth-century bridge we trundled and into the bus station. Out we piled, blinking gawkishly. Up the pavement we charged, turning into St John Street and Glendower Street and arriving with moments to spare. Ushered to sundry classrooms, we sat formally behind desks, wide-eyed with wonderment. You could hardly move for spick-and-span coats and bags. Flushed faces beamed expectantly. We had not long to wait. In came Mr. Senior, a sensible name for a headmaster if ever there was one, and we falteringly stood, making a dreadful din. With a slightly bored gesture he bad us sit. We repeated the racket. Everything fell silent.

"Welcome to Monmouth School. This has been a seat of learning since the year Napier published his famous treatise on logarithms: 1614. And it is a seat of learning today. Strange, you may say, of course a school is such a place - but consider, we are also renowned for our sporting prowess. While here you will make many friends and a few enemies. There are numerous clubs and societies to provide a divertissement. But our *raison d'être* - or, for those unfamiliar with foreign tongues, our reason for existence - is learning. You are arriving ignorant, if you will forgive my bluntness, and you will leave otherwise. You! What's the opposite of 'ignorant'?"

"Guilty, sir," said a dozy object.

"So you are," said Senior, "and we have ways with the guilty here. 'Erudite', my boy - from *erudire* meaning 'to polish'. You will be polished, self-assured men of the world, or nearly so, and certainly ready to meet the world on your terms. How will this happen? Through effort and discipline, primarily on your part. If you do not try, we will make you; if you are unrestrained, we will temper your conduct. Be under no illusion: you are here to work. But you shall be happy. Is that understood?" There was a fair amount of grave nodding and worried agreement. "Good. The staff will answer any questions." We rose loudly. He swept out, gathering his gown about him. He had not been severe. Indeed, his tone had been mild - sort of. We were left in no doubt that those in control knew what they were doing greatly more than we did. Of necessity, all that remained was to observe the school motto: Serve and Obey.

Thereafter, to quote John Milton, all hell broke loose. I moved at 180 paces a minute - at the double. Prefects as big as the Colossus of Rhodes reared then faded. Books rained past. Timetables ensnared. Deadlines loomed. Three minutes to reach such and such a classroom! The edifice was inconceivably old. In comparison The Narth primary school was as modern as yesterday's papers. A gruff voice. A frown. The bell! "Hurry, child, you're late!" I raced off in the wrong direction.

There were thirty staff, males of an age and venerableness I would never attain. Even when older than them I would never be as old as them. They embodied authority the way water embodies wetness. They were marvellously confident and collaborative. I could hardly imagine one at odds with another. Human nature being what it is there were doubtless intrigues and enmities, but these stout-hearted fellows were as one in my eyes: eloquent, imperturbable, intellectual. Only the art, music, and games masters were non-graduates. All had lace-ups and turn-ups and side partings. None shambled or slouched. Most had a quasi-military bearing. Theirs was the generation for whom the cerebral rigours of Wittgenstein were yielding to the celluloid horrors of Frankenstein; in 1956 Hammer Studios remade the original film in colour with added gore. Two World Wars had hardened and honed the communal consciousness. Although the Third Reich was dead its spirit lingered to haunt a bruised and battered Europe. In my first year the Combined Cadet Force was still seemingly on red alert: both the Army section camp at Castlemartin near Pembroke and the Royal Air Force section at Spitalgate near Grantham fairly bristled with martial activity. German was not taught. It was the language of a twice-defeated and humiliated nation.

We sat alphabetically in either 1A or 1B, sixty boys under the obscure heading *Salvete*, ranging from Ballinger G.J. to Woodley B.P. Lessons were acceptable, though it took ages to discover why we had to learn Latin. Report for Michaelmas Term 1958: *A poor exam. He is a slow worker, due mainly to his tendency to daydream.* I was not so much daydreaming as glacially adapting. My best showing that term was in History, the only O level I failed. My worst was in English. *Very weak* pronounced Mr. H.E.R. Gill, a doctor feeling a dying man's pulse. Already it was clear that in my mother tongue I was a no-hoper.

Sport should have provided an escape. Mostly it meant running around and I was used to that. Like any sane hominid, however, I feared pain. Within my admittedly narrow canon of reference unpleasantness was unpleasant and to be avoided. It was unreasonable to argue otherwise, yet weekly we had to, forcing pale, pathetic bodies into games kits and hurrying to bleak expanses where we shivered until our teeth chattered. Rugby's spectrum ranged from Prince Obolensky's legendary tries against the All Blacks in 1936 to 1B snivelling in the rain twenty-two years later. Between these extremes heroes flourished: prop forwards as solid as Martello towers, hookers as agile as ferrets, wing three-quarters as nifty as greased lightning. And was this not the alma mater of John Gwilliam, the captain under whom Wales recorded Grand Slams in 1950 and 1952.

The school was 35% architecture, 35% staff, and 30% pupils in terms of what I found influential. The buildings *brooded*. Nowhere could you find the obscenity of a terrapin. Walls were as durable as forever; floors and doors were solid oak. Whoever built the place entertained long- rather than short- or medium-term considerations. This was intimidating and reassuring in equal measure. The masters were made of the next best thing to seasoned wood: prime beef. None was a milksop. They combined the aura of Pope John XXIII with the indomitable courage of 'Sugar' Ray Robinson, who had recently regained the world middleweight title for the fourth time.

Chapel was an edifice you dashed to and sauntered from. Once there you sat among peers and experienced the enforced spirituality of a hymn, a prayer, and an address. You never got the better of Chapel. It existed before you and promised to continue long after you. You sampled it like cod roe - not to everyone's taste, but reputed to do you good. It was an institution within an institution, and that - school - resided within an institutional Britain. Everything had weight and worth. For the annual carol service we defiled to St. Mary's Gothic nave to worship amid even more auspicious surroundings. The building itself was by no means ancient. G.E. Street designed it around 1880, though a church had stood thereabouts since 1102. My unfulfilled ambition was to enter the organ loft, which seemed holier than the chancel. There pimply bespectacled eggheads played with dazzling dexterity while Mr. Michael Eveleigh conducted the choir. I could not tell a breve from a hemidemisemiquaver yet I managed somehow to inveigle my way into this august body, lasting as treble and alto until an officious bod named

C.W. Herbert, who went on to become Bishop of St Albans, sacked me for lateness.

Forty days after Easter we finished at noon. That morning we warbled:

> *Hail the day that sees him rise,*
> > *Alleluia.*
> *to his throne above the skies;*
> > *Alleluia.*
> *Christ, the Lamb for sinners given,*
> > *Alleluia.*
> *enters now the highest heaven.*
> > *Alleluia.*

This was cheering. If there was a 'highest heaven' there must be lower heavens. All was not lost, for into one of these a second-rater such as I might creep. I slid from 1A to 2B to 3C, from the scholarly to the semiskilled. Had 4D existed I would have been in it. My second report still showed me lowest in English, as did my third. The following year our subject teacher changed from Mr. H.E.R. Gill to Mr. R. Russell Craps. Gill's nickname was Fishy; goodness knows what Craps's was. Few exercise books remain from that period to show why I was so uninspiring. Mostly attitude was to blame: naïve, otherworldly, speculative. Then in 3C something happened. The pace slackened. Tension eased. I was now among hewers of wood and drawers of water, horny-handed sons of toil, striplings from the county's farms - not thick, just practical. Somehow the elements gelled and I rose to eighth position overall, among the top three in Agricultural Science, Chemistry, French, Geography, and History. Dizzy heights indeed.

Puberty started. Itching lichen. Broken voices. We became gangling and combative, nervous and outspoken by turns. The fresh-faced innocent eleven-year-old all but disappeared. In his place stood a lad whose uniform was ill-fitting, whose tie sagged, and whose hair flopped. If he was a dayboy he noticed that girls his age on the school bus had developed bumps under their blouses, lustrous hair, and an assertive way of walking. If he was a boarder his dormitory was no longer merely for sleeping in. It became a breeding ground for bittersweet horseplay and innuendo. Suddenly your thing took on unwonted significance as the site of the five-knuckle shuffle. It had telescopic properties akin to those at Manchester University's Radio Astronomy Laboratories. It made you see stars. Already Cockney rhyming slang talked of Having a Jodrell.

My initiation came unexpectedly during a Divinity lesson. My back-row neighbour produced his prick while the class sat considering the life and times of an early Christian martyr. I stared down at it as if at a dead fish. It was inordinately big, a pike on a tradesman's bench. "Have a feel," he urged with a lascivious grin. I did. It was still alive. '...but because Polycarp, Bishop of Smyrna, refused to recognise false gods, the Roman proconsul threatened him with....' A hand slid across and unbuttoned my fly. This was silly. I brushed it aside and refocused the Reverend W.T. Joseph who was describing the saint's trials and tribulations. The following week the rigmarole resumed. What was he up to? This time I let him handle the goods. It acted like a tonic. Surely this was wrong. What if we were seen? Then I heard that walk-in cupboards at the new teaching block were used for more advanced activities. Apparently it was to do with spermatozoa and testosterone. This sent me to the library. 'Spermatozoa. Name given to the motile microgameti....' Eh? 'Testosterone. Formula: $C^{19} H^{28} O^2$. A steroid hormone whose production at adolescence is controlled by the pituitary, a vascular mass situated in the sella turcica and retained by a process of dura mater.' "Wanking," said my companion friskily. "Ever tried it?"

Monmouth School was far from being a hotbed of vice. What Lord Stonham proclaimed in the mid-sixties - 'During a fairly active life, including 25 years playing team games, I have never encountered homosexuality' - could have applied to anyone with a quarter of a century's experience of this establishment. Third-form frolics were more a matter of perverse curiosity; though swimming lessons were different. The pool was open to the elements, and obligatory forays into its icy depths commenced each summer term. There must have been warmer water-sports in Siberia. I am sure Mr. Glyn John, our Games master, added antifreeze beforehand. Even clad in wet suits we would have been cold; virtually naked, it was almost unbearable. Such extremes produced odd effects. Torsos blanched. Blood concentrated in a protective capacity around vital organs. Eyes reddened, noses ran, fingers showed leprous insensitivity, teeth became castanets. If you could not take it you were a sissy. If you could you were made of titanium and had glycol in your veins. Towelling down afterwards in a changing cubicle with a canvas curtain across the doorway blithely heralded the hauling-on of clothes and escape to temperate classrooms. After school when it was sunny and the water had been warming all afternoon, you could spend forty minutes in the pool voluntarily. This was conducted by rota according to whichever House you were in. Now you bathed with boys of up to eighteen years of age. Some sixth-formers were ultrafriendly and made a point of drying their knackers with studied indifference while facing you. This did weird things to what my dictionary called 'the intromissive organ'. It pointed like Kitchener on a Great War poster. Again I was invited occasionally to feel a propinquitous monstrosity. Whether I did or not made little difference to me, though it unaccountably made a lot to them. One large lad in particular relished my company. I found his attentions tiresome. My own member had vestigial hair about its root. His reared from a luxuriance of undergrowth like a watchtower in the Belgian Congo.

Was not gay spy John Vassall a pupil here from 1938 to 1941? Well, yes, but mostly the school's idiocies were far more routine: deification of the 1st XV, disproportionate affection for the classics, and a hearty C.C.F. Like virtually every paramilitary organisation, this was as farcical as it was devotional. Chaps like me, Harry Beach, and 'Rumble' Thomas regularly ended up on fatigue and were frequently summoned for kit inspection, when some prig or other scrutinised every square inch for irregularity. We would try in vain to stop giggling. This would infuriate the youthful commandant. Finally we would be dismissed as spineless drips. While conformists were engaged in fruitless square-bashing, we mooched around doing odd jobs. This was infinitely preferable. Who were the powers-that-be kidding? One A-bomb and the whole of Monmouthshire would have turned to radioactive dust. Manoeuvres were fun because you skived lessons; otherwise it was irredeemably futile. When brass hats yearly took the salute we paced across part of the playing fields' twenty-five acres to the march from *Scipio* like Grenadier Guardsmen trooping the colour. Even then I could not muster any regimental pride or sense of achievement.

If the inflated oval ball constituted a religion, the hard red ball achieved little more than cult status. Monmouth was not pre-eminently a cricketing school. This did not prevent enthusiasts bashing the thing for all they were worth. There is for some a certain romance in the sound of leather on willow. The main advantage of the one game over the other is that it is less injurious and more restful. Most fielders spend their time standing at ease looking white and wonderful like Seraphim waiting for the pubs to open. The main focus of attention is the dervish running up to bowl as if his life depended on it, and the blade at the other end swiping at the pestilential object as it whizzes towards his ears. The poet Edmund Blunden captured something of its atmosphere:

> *On the green they watched their sons*
> *Playing till too dark to see,*
> *As their fathers watched them once,*
> *As my father once watched me;*
> *While the bat and beetle flew*

On the warm air webbed with dew.

He could have been describing rounders or simply the art of messing about - there is no reference to cricket. What he *is* outlining is continuity. Tradition. Successive generations passively observing in an age (he was writing in 1922) when active service had claimed so many. He is depicting archetypal England, typified by eleven on the sward not fifteen in the mud. It is no surprise that Blunden spent his last decade at Long Melford, Suffolk's stateliest town, famed *inter alia* for the green. Every September its magnificent church, Holy Trinity, holds a Bach Festival. There must be someone somewhere who swears by listening to the exuberant fast movements of the *Brandenburg Concertos* on Discman headphones while watching young whatshisname hit a six, or the tender nobility of the *Violin concerto No. 1 in A minor* against that flutter of applause as Fitzgerald helps us into double figures. You could even apply Italian terms to the average delivery: *adagio, moderato, prestissimo*. None of this rendered it more acceptable to the philistine I was. All-Muggleton could have played Dingley Dell till the cows came home and it would not have turned my head.

Those in the know enthused about Compton and Cowdrey, Graveney and Hutton. They fervently discussed chinamen and googlies, backward short leg and cover drive. I meanwhile had discovered an activity in which you did not need to rise from your chair, never had your teeth knocked out, and triumphed by the application of brain over brawn. It was to change my life. The vision came during lunch hour one damp Thursday. Sandwich nibblers were herded into the Hall and passed their time filling their cheeks like trumpeters and dropping crumbs onto the ancient floor. B.R. Godwin, son of a Cinderford jeweller, agreed to teach me *the game and playe of the chesse*. In no time I had rushed out and bought Harry Golombek's Penguin Handbook on the subject and was avidly reliving the cut and thrust of Anderssen versus Kieseritzky,

London 1851. The names, games, venues, and dates seemed shot through with radiance.

Being beside the Wye, the school maintained a rowing tradition. It would have been inept not to have done so. This was best suited to those who could spend evenings getting dizzy and damp from outdoor exertion. Having to race for a late-afternoon bus meant that dayboys whose parents had no car - a relatively high number in the early sixties - missed out on extramural activities, from involvement with the school play to violin lessons with Mr. Hardulak. Clubs and societies existed to counter boarders' boredom. Train spotters chugged along to the Rail Enthusiasts' Club, ping-pongists bounced off to the Table Tennis Club, and assorted bloods convened for Union Society debates. I would be at home, slaving over prep. Electricity reached the village in 1958, and by 1961 most houses had television. Sony had just developed the all-transistor receiver which sounded the knell for those cumbersome sets containing thermionic valves. Our mono-chrome marvel was silent for much of the time, mostly flashing into life for news broadcasts. The day Sir Thomas Beecham died the first U.S. Polaris nuclear submarine gained Holy Loch. We were entering a less gentlemanly age.

As tough sports were denied me by dint of their nature, and as I had to do *something*, I approached the armoury and asked about shooting, having been told that all you had to do was lie still, support a fairly heavy object, and flex your forefinger. This did not sound too difficult. A stuffed shirt looked me up and down. What was my C.C.F. rank? What was my latest tally of tries or runs? Had I represented the school in the Bewdley, Llandaff, or Saltford Regattas?

"Speak up, boy!" he boomed imperiously, though hardly a year my senior.

"If I'm hopeless they'll kick me out. At least give me a chance." He sighed, and nodded sourly.

There was to be ·22 practice indoors and ·303 among the buttercups, Inter-House Competitions, Postal Matches, and Home and Away fixtures. At last I had found a niche, a relaxed caper which - despite making the most noise - few noticed. One reason was that it happened either in the basement range or two miles away near the village of Rockfield. There, in open country, facing the lowering outline of King's Wood, we blasted at distant targets, taking turns to do butts duty. This entailed trudging to frames hoisted from a safety trench, sticking markers through bullet-holes, and signalling bulls, inners, magpies, outers, and misses. We reclined on turf banks, ears stuffed and terrestrial telescopes poised to espy the accuracy of our handiwork, and pleasantly passed countless afternoons. Then I heard we were to camp in broomy coniferous Surrey at a place called Bisley.

I had never been to this far land, reputedly south of London. Having recently discovered the poet John Betjeman, I was aware of its existence and something of its nature. We meandered through market towns en route, there being no motorway yet to shorten our journey. Eventually our coach reached a vast American Civil War encampment with splendid pavilions and khaki jeeps. In the distance dull shots rang out. Flags flapped from tall poles. Trees stood to attention. Even the grass grew with military precision. We passed our first night under canvas soundly enough. Next morning, intent on number twos, I threaded between innumerable guy-lines towards what was ostensibly a latrine. A row of twelve sizeable holes in a broad wooden unit lay open to the sky. The shock made finding a good old-fashioned jakes the more necessary.

Bisley reminded me that public-school boys were not a dying breed. The world was full of them. Moreover they came from places whose names rang a bell - Ampleforth, Charterhouse, Milton Abbey, Stowe... whereas I was sure few had heard of us. What was everybody doing? Aiming to please, literally. Piercing the breeze which set pennants flying as if at a medieval tournament. Tenting one's fingers and waiting one's turn where camaraderie met rivalry. In the evening, the sky a mauve haze, we would go into Guildford and wander about, each with a flagon of cider, feeling lordly and increasingly mellow. I remember chatting up a couple of young women at the station while waiting to return. They said things like *Isn't it past your bedtime?* and *Whose little boy are you then?* Already I was developing a priapic ache for the opposite sex. The possibility of love was even then in the air.

Whenever we visited Bisley we did not underachieve. Some of us scored creditably on Ashburton Day and won Gale and Polden 1963 centenary mugs. The following summer I escaped to Aldershot one evening and saw the film of the moment: a quartet of mopheads behaving wackily in places such as Paddington Station, the Scala Theatre in Charlotte Street W1, and St Margaret's Field near Gatwick. *A Hard Day's Night* was all I hoped it would be and more besides. I had thought it might simply be a glossy promo for the fab four. I should have known better.

My geology O level was unreservedly satisfying. As the examination clashed with Bisley, several of us sat it at Cranleigh, the nearest school timetabled for the subject. The morning was agreeable, the building imposing, and the surrounding countryside attractive. Any doubts were quickly dispelled; it was one of the few such ordeals I actually enjoyed. We returned along leafy lanes in a drophead coupé which had hide seats, a walnut dash, and glinting chrome. High above, fat clouds grinned like washerwomen up to their elbows in suds. I had never realised identifying ammonites could be such fun.

For numerous reasons we failed to be overall winners in competition. We settled inexorably at our predicted level, consoling ourselves with the also-ran's perennial let-out: 'It's only a game'. Individuals occasionally fluked but none matched the consistency of the Williamson brothers from Ross-on-Wye. Love them or hate them, you had to admit this duo had steely nerves coupled with uncanny vision and achieved regularly what others scored with frustrating infrequency. My only prize at Monmouth was for winning a contest I did not realise I had entered. Mr. F.R.H. Elgood was seeking fresh woods and pastures new and donated an engraved silver spoon to the Rifle Club to commemorate his departure. In a related test of marksmanship, which I took to be just another practice session, I achieved the target score, beating the accomplished twosome. The headmaster, Mr. R.F. Glover, awarded me the trophy in front of a disbelieving audience. As we shook hands he muttered the three most laudatory words I was to hear during my entire seven years at Monmouth: "Well done, George." I smiled, thanked him, and returned to a sitting ovation. Speech Days were flowery occasions with marquees, boaters, and vol-au-vents, when achievers lightened the guest speaker's table of its bookish load. Not for me *The Seven Pillars of Wisdom* by T.E. Lawrence, Orwell's *Burmese Days*, or Thackeray's *Esmond* - only the Elgood Spoon… and applause which should have been a shade faster.

A few gowned gods had wished me well in my chosen career as O levels came to a close, a none-too-subtle way of saying they did not expect to see me around for A levels. They were to be proved wrong. But which A levels? Having no particular ambition, I drifted into art, economics, and geography. The only subjects I *loved* at school, chemistry and French, were ones you were not allowed to pursue by themselves. The next two years were a glorious waste of time spent making tea and toast in prefectorial studies and missing lessons, many of which my associates and I deemed grotty. Thus we gained lamentable examination grades. Parents fumed. Where was that passe-partout to the Establishment: entry to Balliol or King's? All right, Bangor or Bradford or Strathclyde - anywhere other than the scrapheap of a polytechnic or the backwater of teacher training?

"Your father's livid. You should hang your head in shame. You'll never get to be anyone now."

I begged to differ. "Winston Churchill did badly at school, didn't he."

Mother fixed me with a stern eye. "You get born in Blenheim Palace, *you* can do badly," she intoned like a dyspeptic Yiddisher momma.

Edward Breitenberger was affecting my hair. His stage name was Edd Byrnes and he was the *77 Sunset Strip* hipster who was forever slicking his quiff. He was sunny, streetwise, and able to leap from supine to vertical like reversed film. Our study walls sported photographs of such characters. We were victims of media hype, as were the media themselves. We assumed that knowing Chas Chandler played bass guitar for The Animals would secure us a plum job with the Atomic Energy Authority; telling the loco-motion from the mashed potato would ease us into the Ministry of Defence Procurement Executive; doing a passable rendition of Roy Orbison's *It's Over* would lead to directorships at Asprey & Co. of Bond Street. Er, no. What might, conceivably, was studying the national debt, the balance of payments, and John Maynard Keynes. Why had our parents not been stricter? Why had they embodied such a *laissez-faire* attitude? Why had they not clipped our wings? Lenin was right when he said liberty is so precious it should be rationed.

Pals from The Narth rarely consorted with me after the eleven-plus; those who had passed were automatically regarded as stuck-up. Colin Saunders, a classmate from the nearby village of Llanishen, became a close acquaintance, especially as we holidayed as part of the same group twice: at Watcombe in Devon, and at Penmaenmawr in Caernarvonshire. Our guide on both occasions was his priest, an enigmatic celibate with a penchant for king-size cigarettes. Susan Coombs was the fifteen-year-old daughter of a couple my parents had recently befriended. She and I and the other youngsters left Newport for Torquay aboard a compartment train in which we faced a few fellow travellers, gazed through the window, or scanned scenes of postwar Britain above the buttoned antimacassars: Arthur's Seat, Beachy Head, Bridlington Bay.... We intended to stay a fortnight. Within a week the cream had soured. She and an associate failed to return from an evening stroll, having met two lads and not noticed how late it was getting. The police were called and the minors found and given their marching orders. Next morning they were unceremoniously dumped on the Bristol express and sent packing. So much for the New English Bible *New Testament*, published the previous year to much ballyhoo. 'Be generous to one another, tender-hearted, forgiving one another as God in Christ forgave you' was its rendering of Ephesians 4 : 2, a verse with which our padre was unacquainted. Nowadays their peccadillo would merit a warning. Then it assumed genocidal proportions. Thereafter the days passed pleasantly enough. Apart from a few teddy boys trespassing in order to ogle the talent, nothing untoward happened. Also minding us were the Vicar of Mitchel Troy and a mandatory lady who dealt with girls' affairs, which we took to mean the dispensation of sanitary towels.

Undaunted by our exploits, several of us - under the ambiguous gaze of the red-faced bachelor cleric - journeyed to North Wales twelve months later, this time from Hereford. A nasal Tannoy at Crewe echoed above our hurry to change trains; a cheer sounded on glimpsing the Dee estuary; then it was Prestatyn, Rhyl, Colwyn Bay, Conway, and our destination. We tumbled onto the gusty platform, tingling with anticipation. The previous summer had been enlivened by the prominence of Frank Ifield's hit single *I Remember You*, Pat Boone's *Speedy Gonzales*, and Bobby Darin's *Things*. Now The Searchers' *Sweets for my Sweet*, Billy J. Kramer's *Bad to Me*, and Buddy Holly's *Wishing* sounded from every jukebox. Gulls wheeled raucously overhead. Waves advanced and retreated, a drunk on a sloping pavement. What you noticed about the town's backdrop was its steepness: 1,500 feet of soaring solemnity being quarried slowly and shipped by coaster from the jetty. Gladstone loved the place and so did we. Soon a pretty young thing named Christine materialised.

How mature to travel unchaperoned! A few evenings

later we trundled off with some local girls, this one included, to Conway. The town, whose walls were six feet thick, boasted Britain's smallest house, Wales's oldest house, and a magnificent castle dating from 1283. Soon we were ambling effervescently along compact streets, hardly noticing the Elizabethan, Jacobean, Georgian, and Victorian architecture. What counted more than fishing boats, lobster creels, and gift shops was her hand in mine and the radiance of her face. Pleasure craft bobbed at anchor; a mulberry dark descended; lights twinkled about us. At the end of the evening we returned over the points and past saluting signalling equipment, thundering through tunnel and beside beach and road. The window's reflection showed a teenage couple cuddling awkwardly. Suddenly there was a critical juncture as our lips met, small and moist, against the rhythmic reverberations of the carriage. Brakes were applied, and it slid to a halt. Doors banged, and we rose - shaking slightly - and got off.

This led to more togetherness, inevitable goodbyes, and an exchange of letters which petered out after two years. The minutiae-filled billets-doux expressed hope and uncertainty. David from Birkenhead asks you to go with him; you say no but he will not take no for an answer; you and a girl-friend pile into his car and a group of you end up at Holyhead. I say if anyone checks they will find the table-tennis bat one of us chucked through a ceiling trapdoor when staying at the Old School, now your youth club. You say Sir Michael Duff will shortly present you with a pre-nursing certificate. I say the Beatles' Cheltenham concert on Friday 1st November has, alas, sold out. You say you have left school to work as a dressmaker. I mention my forthcoming holiday job at Servite House, Ealing, a Roman Catholic home for the disabled. You state your latest height and weight. I bemoan looming examinations. You say your maiden name will change from Aughton when you marry Trevor on your eighteenth birthday. The correspondence stops. Inexplicably I still have the *Daily Express* cutting from December 1963 showing Jan Papluhar, centre half for Slovan Bratislava, signing autographs for you and fellow pupils at Aberconwy School.

5

Holiday romances can fade with the rapidity of drying ink. Frequent renewal of stimulus is needed. Lads like me should, my father reckoned, consort with the opposite sex rather than with sonnets and sestinas or the chess games of Steinitz. As he considered such pursuits unhealthy compared with courting, the relationship with my Devon-holiday companion Susan was expected to blossom. Our parents got on well with hers; and she was a bright creature, clean, attractive, with just a hint of plumpness. They lived in a large solid house overlooking a common in the village of Bream. Sheep roamed freely beyond the front gate, a familiar sight in the Forest of Dean. She attended Bell's Grammar School in Coleford, and had no siblings.

I enjoyed the spiritedness of her letters. She wrote as she spoke, producing ideal sentiments for that time and place, voicing the kind of urgent platitude which necessarily wanes with adulthood. 'It's sheer hell without you. I'm writing this in bed. Wish you were here. PS When you reply use those three words every girl longs for. PPS Goodnight and God Bless.' Soon we were weekending together, dutifully taxied hither and thither by doting adults. Did they have something long-term in mind? Had I not been uprooted by a year's nursing, then three years' further education, the answer might have been yes - though a silly disagreement was to cool their ardour, if not ours. So I shelved prosody and opening theory in favour of long walks and convoluted talks. One of her postscripts astutely read: 'Whatever you do, keep away from blooming psychoanalysis, dear, you'll drive everyone absolutely bonkers'. Some discussions veered heavily towards sexual imagery and dream interpretation, enough to try the patience of any healthy sixteen-year-old virgin. With a nudge and a wink I'd murmur, "Guess what Sigmund Freud thought cigars signify". Oh, the subtlety! "Did you know, according to him apples symbolise breasts?" Why did she put up with it? Probably because she had a sturdy sense of humour. Like most adolescent females, she was more in love with the idea of love than with flesh and blood: like most such males, I was more in love with flesh and blood than with any high-flown concept. Through Parkhill Inclosure, the wood near her home, we wandered hand in hand, embroiled in juicy discourse. She had scored her satchel with my name and chosen Ronnie Carroll's sugary 1962 single *Roses Are Red* as 'our song'. As I was at a single-sex establishment and had no exhibitionistic sister, my curiosity about the female form became mildly frenetic. The frustrations of proximity bedazzled. I ached to fondle her russets or to light a phallic Havana.

She found such concerns more suited to a comedy film. Slap and tickle always were the wrong way round. To one who has never petted it can seem rum. There you are, a decade and a half from the cradle, having run the gauntlet of childhood, alone on a sofa with a boy your age. He will not play with a train set or your dolls, snakes and ladders, or ludo. He wants to feel inside your dress. Do you let him? What is the point? He would be better off in the Scout Association if he craves adventure. Klondike prospectors could pan a fortune from rapid streams, but knickers never yielded gold nuggets; whatever he strikes cannot be rushed to the assayer's office and tipped onto the scales. The more she chortled dismissively the more I barked like a dog demanding walkies. With tired detachment, she finally relented. "Very well." I sat up straight in disbelief. "If it'll make you happy," she conceded with a yawn. A hermit crab crawled up the smooth skin of her thigh. Eventually it reached a mollusc shell and reconnoitred its new habitat. "Tell me when you've finished," she said with the same jejune air. "Don't you feel anything?" I asked. "Of course," she snapped, "what d'ya expect?" The intruder reappeared and rested on her knee. She sprang from the sofa, walked to the window, and lifted a hard green apple, which she disfigured with one voracious bite. With her other hand (and a shade distractedly, I thought) she flipped open a *Family Circle* and started reading. Admittedly my experience of women was limited, yet even I imagined they would swoon with rapture after a massage in the mystic grotto. Not a bit of it. This set me thinking. Did not the art of seduction demand a relaxed atmosphere rather than blind groping? Those admen knew a thing or two. Where was romance? Where was Mantovani and his shimmering strings? Sex was not catch-as-catch-can, it was spider and fly, the beaux' stratagem.

Next time I visited I chose not to wear underpants. Unfortunately all my trousers buttoned rather than zipped. With practice I managed to get their opening down to a few seconds. Even if I did not expose my nuts and bolt she would surely feel them when she sat on my lap. What a ruse! She sat on my lap. Her weight obscured their presence. Not even I could feel them. Back to the drawing board. Ah, the ultimate tactile treat. Clinch. Kiss. Guide her digits downwards. It was the only remaining ploy. She sat on my lap. We kissed. I redirected her hand. She resisted. Eventually she touched the long barrow, a hesitant archaeologist at a Neolithic mound. I hoped no diversionary *Family Circle* was near. However, she went no further, saying she wanted me primarily for my mind. Our nearest approach to what the French call *la petite mort* was once when she came to stay. After supper as we sat on the sofa watching the box I slipped my hand down the front of her elasticated skirt. The room was dark. Father snored softly. Mother too was nodding. My right middle finger caressed her gently. She became unusually heated. Had we been in bed it would have been magic. Just then the old boy stirred, rubbed his eyes, and stretched. I disengaged, and she went off the boil.

Why did I want to do this so much? Why did she mostly want to stop me without providing a suitable alternative? Perhaps she feared getting in the pudding club. Had we harnessed my curiosity I might have become a successful gynaecologist at, say, the Royal Free Hospital or Bart's. As regards human warmth and fondness we had no scope beyond what was allowed. Parents avowedly knew best. They had money: we had hand-outs. They slept together nightly: we were kept moving, prisoners in an exercise yard. Where there were soft surfaces and coverings we were rarely left unattended. Quilt rhymed with guilt, wooing with undoing, amorous suavity with glamorous depravity. What was nice became a vice. You could not get away from the bad shadow goodness threw, from innocence's alter ego. I still have a lock of her hair. I cannot discard it because, like a nursery book, it is a tangible relic of a past which has gone forever. This is why antiques and museum exhibits are more enlivening than essays, however eloquent, on related themes. One mourns the passing of calf love for its bittersweet absurdity, its thrilling hesitancy, though ultimately it lacks a satisfactory edge. Mothers and fathers stand in the wings while you are urged downstage to ad-lib hopefully and hopelessly, to advance until twenty fingertips *just* touch. You recoil with surprise. The watchers smirk. You begin again.

So, my darling, I did not worship you nor did you worship me - despite scented paper assurances of undying devotion. We needed each other, if only to rival our friends' juvenile infatuations. Had it been true love I would have perished from grief, Tristan to your Isolde, and you would have committed felo de se, spotlighted against a Wagnerian chorus as the curtain descended. Instead, as suddenly as my overweening father had decided we should start courting he decided we should stop. Or, put another way, the Montagues and Capulets had drawn wooden swords and I no longer had a balcony to address. Nonetheless, the cynicism of reappraisal cannot dull that remembered expectancy, when life was a guessing game, both in terms of future spouse and future occupation. Before the sixties were out she had become pregnant by someone else and to this day lives two miles from the scene of our teenage flirtation. It remains difficult to know how much importance to attach to such personal reminiscences. Duisburg alone has half a million inhabitants, many with comparable memories. Anyhow, like Capulet at the masque, 'You and I are past our dancing days'. It is time to put aside doubts, yearnings, and speculation on what might have been until old age lets parallel lines converge to yield an appropriate perspective.

6

I spent from September 1965 to August 1966 working at the Royal Gwent Hospital, Newport. With a white uniform buttoned nattily along one shoulder, I felt like an acned Dr. Kildare. Most irksome of these facial phenomena were persistent Popocatépetls which erupted near the corners of my mouth. This was attributable to the fact that I had stopped using soap because a magazine article said it destroyed the skin's natural oils. Ablutions thereafter consisted of a cowboy's splash of the jowls. That within days my face appeared to be sculpted from lard failed to register with my parents. They probably put the glaze down to the mysteries of late adolescence.

It took the whole of being eighteen to realise nursing was not for me. The surprise was that it was for anyone. After emerging relatively unscathed from a minor public school, here I was stumbling into the profession my half-sister and mother had entered. The difference was that women had access to the priceless facility of a nurses' home. Being potential rapists, my gender were excluded, though in fact I was hardly up to molesting a sandfly. It was the other way about: had I received accommodation *my* modesty might have been at peril. Any entomologist will tell you female sandflies are notorious blood-suckers. The answer was to seek digs. Some were found half a mile away at 24 Clytha Square. There I passed three hundred exhausted nights. Mornings were spent dashing around wards armed with a stainless-steel shield. From what did this brandished bedpan protect you? The answer was a monstrous sluice with a seemingly inexhaustible appetite.

Having ploughed my A levels with sufficient thoroughness to merit a rosette at an agricultural show, I had to do something redemptive - namely, get a job. And as jobs, according to an ethos absorbed through long years of middle-class education, were for plebs, a profession was needed. Being too lily-livered to follow my father into the police force, which he had left on a stretcher, I chose medicine. Arab stallions elsewhere were bearing their riders to doctorates and consultancies; for me an asinine career spent stitching up drunks and pandering to the elderly seemed imminent. Had the wages been adequate, even now I might be laying out some nonagenarian - but they were not. Paying for lodgings and weekly return bus fare left five pounds with which to impress the girls. Despite the relative cheapness of living then, the sum would not provide a down-payment on the Ferrari Lusso of my dreams, nor promise a Lutyens-designed residence near Petworth.

Not that existence lacked compensations. The first six weeks were a continuation of school, with naïve girls as companions instead of sporty boys who beneath their abrasive exterior had been every bit as naïve. Constantly I was reminded of the perfume counter at Boots rather than the changing rooms at Monmouth. The hegemony of jockstraps had yielded to the tentative outline of brassieres. Lessons, now called lectures and delivered by stern matronly figures, took place in a rambling building high above town near the junction of Friars Road and Belle Vue Lane, convenient for both the Royal Gwent and St. Woolos Hospital. Its inhabitants were a cheery warden, a grinning skeleton, and several resuscitation mannequins whom no kiss of life would ever revive. Most fellow students were as colourful as putty, pencil-sucking valley girls who had also, perhaps, demonstrated insufficient A-level ability. Here testing was to be a way of life, frying pan and fire again proving collusive.

As my home had only a bath, most of the showers I had taken had come straight from the sky, hence my enthusiasm for the Preliminary Training School's facilities. After a gruelling day spent surviving Boots' perfumes and learning about myocardial infarctions, I would slope off to a cubicle and soap away the blues while humming the likes of Barry McGuire's *Eve of Destruction*. Early one evening the washroom door banged open and a group of freshers burst in, appropriated my somewhat grubby accoutrements, and marched out. Flabbergasted, I hopped down the passage clad only in a threadbare towel, to discover my sacred Y-fronts being tossed from one to another at the top of the stairs. A teenage harridan, some fearless future warrior who would doubtless strike dread into the hearts of innumerable patients, appeared to be the ringleader, if only on account of her braying laugh. An exhibitionist reduced to bare essentials might have relished tiptoeing around on cold linoleum viewed from above by a chorus of Furies. He might even have let slip the fateful covering. For that he would have needed something worthwhile to exhibit. Shock and chill had reduced my manhood to insignificant proportions; a dropped towel would have provided corroboration for those who considered the teaching block short on freak phenomena. Along with a scattering of pickled embryos and eyeballs, why not a shrivelled specimen of male sexuality? Thankfully it never got to that. Everything went black and I found myself under a heap of clothes. I scampered back, dressed without drying, climbed through a window, and escaped to my sombre bachelor pad.

The hospital routine was generally unexciting. Much of it seemed to consist of hurrying along miles of corridor, frequently at unsocial hours. What did I expect: Club Mediterranée? I never really knew what I was doing. Like some fresh-faced stormtrooper, I just followed orders. Had a stiff-necked Kommandant, with manic visage and barking voice, told me to put an old dear out of her misery I would have done so. Had he suggested I give a bronchitic a Woodbine or a diabetic a stick of barley sugar I would have followed his instruction to the letter.

Meanwhile the sixties were swinging healthily. My haircut proved it. Even the uniform looked gear with its severe round neckline and buttons from armpit to waist. Yet London could have been on another planet. There was hardly time to watch television; and if the miniskirt was raising blood pressures, people like me were doling out drugs to lower them. Julie Christie was making every doctor wish his surname were Zhivago; I was urging zonked-out businessmen to swallow their mephentermine. Wrong again. Mephentermine *raises* blood pressure. Small wonder there was a breezy turnover in bed occupancy on whichever ward I worked. Perhaps it was that fashionable fringe and Martian garb. Seen in a particular light stalking dark-eyed and sallow-cheeked down the centre of the ward, I might have convinced many their time had come and an alien was about to disconnect their drip. However, the spectre of manslaughter failed in turn to haunt me, and the months motored by like Jim Clark's Lotus Climax. Crashing out of harness at 8.30 p.m., some of my colleagues anticipated a riotous evening. For me it meant curling up with a good book and trying to keep awake to the foot of the page. And all for five quid a week! Altruism had to be my motive. At this rate I would soon assume the emaciated proportions of Mahatma Gandhi.

My only male colleague was Paul Pimm, a dapper individual adept at the acoustic guitar. I marvelled at his dexterity. He had the natural ease of Andres Segovia coupled with boyish good looks. I wondered why he did not have his own TV show. Was replacing cardboard sputum-pots really preferable? Would not aeons spent in the black hole of this infirmary deaden his senses and queer his perfect pitch? As he lived in Newport he could retire after a hard day's night to practise. Plectrum or finger-picking: neither presented any difficulty; his digits flashed over the strings like spiders spinning traceries at velocities approaching that of light. How I coveted his skill, which seemed wasted in pursuit of pure sound. I would have used this musical legerdemain to attract pretty aphids into my web. This was, after all, the age of Elvis Presley and James Bond posing amid worshipful recumbent females. I could only ape the banshee with a harmonica, hardly a suitable means by which to advertise my charms.

My landlady, Jane Rowlands, had a shadowy though probably innocuous past and had until recently worked at the local branch of WH Smith. She was a considerate and amiable companion. Her most acerbic comment during my tenancy was "What's wrong with your legs?" Surprised, I had replied, "Nothing, why?" Her steady gaze made me review what I had just said. She had prepared a culinary delight from a Heinz tin and placed it in front of me, having already devoured hers. In mid-sentence I had cavalierly asked for a bottle of Worcester sauce, hence her shattering riposte. Humbled, I traipsed off to get some from the pantry.

The most tedious shift, apart from night duty, was 8.00 a.m. to 2.00 p.m. then 4.30 p.m. to 8.30 p.m. What was so sadistic about this was the modicum of freedom mid-afternoon: time enough for a spot of ocean racing perhaps or the tossing-off of a Gothic novel. My virginal peers ransacked Woolworth's for Biros and foolscap paper: I wandered Belle Vue Park, across the way from our lecture rooms, composing adolescent tosh, poesy in the spirit of Dylan Thomas at his beloved Cwmdonkin Park.

What of other pursuits? Surely there were japes, shrieks, giggles, and hoydenish high spirits. No. Or if yes, not within my ambit. When I was not asking Jane for sauce or sitting, embowered, penning odes to my nail clippings I was mooching forlornly about town, occasionally seeking refuge in a smoky bar. Commercial Road was my beat. It *smelt* different. Bombay duck, chutneys ranging in taste from boot polish to battery acid, curries which could skin your tongue, okra like Pharaonic fingers: all went for a song. Men peed in the street at chucking-out time; ladies of the night loitered, spent and consumptive; flea-bitten dogs receded down rubbish-strewn alleyways. It had character. Dockland pubs possessed a coarse grandeur the well heeled would never stumble upon, a seamy realism that made *Coronation Street* look stagy.

The hospital had a ruling triumvirate, three wise sisters of advanced years, one of whom was Matron. None had a hair out of place. They appeared meek; on closer inspection the meekness was preciseness; head-on the preciseness was steeliness. A narrowing of the eyes by any of them could have felled an ox. To incur their displeasure was akin to ruffling a Mafia boss: he might smile and adjust his tie clip but next morning you would find yourself in the Hudson River wearing concrete slippers. The nearest I came to a 2 a.m. visit was after I had left my lunch companions in the staff refectory and, dabbing my mouth with a paper napkin, made for the door. Hardly the Crime of the Century you might think; if you did three wise sisters would disabuse you. The rule, I learned, was no one *ever* rose from the table before they did. It betokened the utmost discourtesy. That explained the afternoon call for someone with my name. I took it. A thin voice emanating from the celestial ether told me the next time I left lunch prematurely I would be dealt with severely. Although a lethal injection was not mentioned you could tell it was on the cards. I apologised from the depths of an aggrieved innocence and replaced the receiver.

Having never attempted O level mathematics I took private lessons with a local teacher. Weekly I trekked to his study after work to master positive and negative numbers, graphical representation, formulae, equations…. I virtually sat on his lap while he patiently showed how to manipulate figures for the common good. It all made uncommon sense. I exited walking on my hands, the room contracting and expanding like a mad lens. If I did not follow this loopy track they would not accept me for teacher training, which was what I realised would be a more remunerative proposition than nursing.

When first-year examinations arrived I did particularly well, mainly through mirroring my examiners' prejudices. In written papers I regurgitated lecture notes verbatim. To mark me down would have been to negate their own teaching; therefore, with tasteful diagrams and dulcet sentences in a legible script, I performed with pleasing rectitude. What bothered me about this approach was its lack of scope for originality: surely ulcers could as easily be described in iambic pentameter, or varicose veins in the style of James Joyce. The only grey matter of which they wanted evidence was the patient's. So my fountain pen, which cocked its little leg like a pooch every time you filled it, rolled on over the undemanding pages. Practical tests were less successful. Girls are more used to household chores, whether they should be or not, and most fellow students could have made beds to perfection bound and gagged. With all limbs fully functional, I could not match their seamless excellence. Tutors frowned as I reduced some old boy to gooseflesh while washing him, or maladministered an enema with four pints of hot water and a yard of rubber tubing. This and my confident smirk must have made me seem like a bent emcee at a Hamburg nightclub. Others had spent scores of hours patching up teddy bears from the age of three. Paul Pimm and I had not. Thus my clove-hitch slings hampered blood supply, and my Tubegauz head bandages caused asphyxiation. Although this was by definition a learning situation and nobody expected you to excel first time, they did by time eleven. From the corner of my eye I could sense clipboard-toting overseers crossing not ticking in the relevant columns; nonetheless, an inane grin still informed my features. The word might eventually get about that the lanky male in this year's intake was a giggling psychopath. The advantage of humour was that when things went wrong you could blame the mood: to play it straight meant it was invariably the perpetrator who was culpable. As it was only a matter of life and death, I thought these initial hiccups would soon blow over. This was misguidedly optimistic. A spasmodic diaphragm does not blow anywhere.

Three miles east of Newport, the college of education at Caerleon overlooked the village. Hereabouts in A.D. 80 the 2nd Augustan Legion established a stronghold of 6000 troops, probably because the watering holes were so good. Pork pies and crisps, Scotch eggs and Welsh bitter: what more could a homesick standard-bearer or morose centurion want? The Romans had gone but the pubs had not; and when I hesitantly arrived, set square and protractor in hand to do battle with hostile numbers, the first thing I learned from an engaging youth as I waited in the corridor for my qualifying test was that anyone who thirsted after knowledge could do no better than come to Caerleon, only forget about the knowledge. As I sat to unravel ninety minutes' worth of algebraic, arithmetic, and geometric knots, a detached area of my consciousness focused an heraldic beast of stunning proportions, tongue hanging out. This Johannine vision resolved itself into Britain's commonest pub sign, the Red Lion, despite having more than a dash of Celtic full-bloodedness, what with its arrowhead tail and tongue, bat's-wing ears, and talons. Dragon or lion: either way the next three years might witness the consumption of an enormous amount of wallop if these pages of tortuous abstraction yielded the correct results.

They did, and in September 1966 I entered this university of the liver with a parched anticipation and a doubter's trepidation. What if my confidant had been mistaken? What if beer and skittles, dances and romances were exception not rule? Worse, what if everything was run by a triumvirate of dour provincial killjoys who did not let you rise from the table until they had finished their own unenlivening gruel? I shuddered. *Come on, boyo,* whispered a jocular phantom voice, *everything will be right as rain, you wait and see.*

I had managed to extricate myself from nursing by convincing the powers that be of my insolvency. There was insufficient recompense for exhaustion. Furthermore, I found the body exercised greatly more than the mind, despite lectures on laryngectomies or lymphoblastic leukaemia. Actually there were few of these; the level of instruction for idealistic valley girls, lank poetasters, and guitar virtuosi was rudimentary. Medical students at the Radcliffe Infirmary or Addenbrookes were into the inspirational meatiness of real therapeutics; we were nibbling around the edges, lost in a maze of mundane chores such as shaving senile cheeks, clearing away half-eaten meals, and hanging Xmas decorations. Real anatomy and physiology were a different world. The average nurse was better acquainted with tidying lockers than with contemplating metacarpophalangeal articulations. As regards social demarcation, hierarchical distinctions existed to an extent comparable with the armed forces. A cross section of hospital life showed as much stratification as Lulworth Cove: a place for everyone and everyone in their place. College would provide a delicious melting pot of attitudes and foibles, with nobody's life hanging by a thread and no soiled sheets to bother about. Yes, there would be bodily secretions but they would prove surprisingly pleasurable. For the time being it was simply a case of shaking hands with the skeleton and wishing everyone else a fond farewell - including two particular tutors, a husband and wife team, the former of whom once gave me a venomous dressing-down for offering him a toffee. I had been catching my breath after an especially gruelling morning and had retired to the sister's office to check a file and have a quick cuppa. Then I committed the heinous error. Among the regulations of the National Board for Nursing, Midwifery and Health Visiting for Wales must somewhere lie the immutable command 'Thou shalt not during the hours of labour proffer any sweetmeat or kindred delicacy to any colleague, preceptor, or patient without prior approval from this body or a delegated representative'. I had no such chitty, hence the bollocking. So farewell, Aesculapian treadmill. *Au revoir,* Clytha Square. *Arrivederci,* glaucoma. And bureaucratic stuffiness, goodbye.

7

In 1249 William of Durham bequeathed £206 14s 4d for the maintenance of ten Masters of Arts at University College, Oxford, making it the oldest such seat of learning in England. Eight years later Robert de Sorbon founded the Collegium Pauperum Magistrorum in Paris. At Cambridge, Massachusetts in 1636 the colony's general court instituted the senior centre of academic excellence in North America. Two years later they named it after John Harvard, who left to it his library and half his estate. These and other prime athletic edifices are way ahead of the rest of the field, the race has been on for some time, and the leaders have been cheered to the echo. Just as bystanders pack up to go home they see, panting in the distance, a warped diminutive figure shambling towards them. An inquisitive soul lifts his binoculars, focuses, and relays to his companions the legend on the pathetic creature's sweatshirt. *Caerleon College of Education.* A whoop goes up, and amid the amused hubbub can be heard urgings of genuine sympathy: "Come on, sunshine - you can make it...".

The first thing we freshers wanted to do was decide what the first thing we wanted to do was: have a plate of chips in the reverberating canteen, or choose which subjects to read during the next three years. I went for brain over stomach. "Drama," someone was earnestly telling someone else, "is all about plays - you know, those things they do on a stage." Other voices vied for attention. "Go on, take a dekko at History. Everyone likes to find out where they came from." Elsewhere a balding middle-aged lecturer was trying to persuade a pretty eighteen-year-old to join his course. "But what does it entail?" she asked innocently. "Oh, very little labour and lots of enjoyment," came the assured reply. "Okay," she responded, running a hand vivaciously through her hair. Her recruiter smiled darkly.

A trendy menopausal dame approached me with the vital question.

"Um, well, I was thinking about Drama...."

She brightened, inching closer, a hen about to gather an errant chick under her wing. "And what might you know of that subject?" she clucked.

I flushed. "It's something which happens on a stage."

Delighted by my perspicacity, she decided there and then this would do. "Welcome to my course," she beamed, extending a beefy hand.

I nodded instead of accepting such committal physicality. Matriculation had been as painless as extracting a corpse's tooth. Soon we might lurch across the boards declaiming 'A horse! a horse! my kingdom for a horse!' Not yet though. It was time for that plate of chips.

The previous afternoon I and my parents had rooted through the suburban estate to the rear of this awesome establishment seeking student accommodation. First-year hopefuls competed for anywhere to lay their head, hostels being denied them for the initial twelvemonth. Like Mary and Joseph plodding from No Vacancy sign to No Vacancy sign, we were about to give up and find a stable when a couple in Lodge Road provided welcome hospitality. He was a blue-collar worker at St Cadoc's psychiatric hospital and a man of such extreme mildness as to make your average weather forecaster seem fierce. She, a jolly bundle of neuroses, was addicted to the smoking of high-tar cigarettes. Their daughter Denise took after her father so far as inoffensiveness was concerned. Their home (I had the main front bedroom) was immaculate. Their lifestyle matched, down to the mandatory bedtime cocoa sipped reverently in front of the television. Their attitude was both liberal and conservative: I could come in at any time, without bringing along friends; I could use their house as if it were my own, without leaving evidence of having done so. I failed them only when heavy-footedly running upstairs. Occasionally my ascent sounded for all the world like a Newport County training session on an expanse of galvanised sheeting.

Back at the hub of intellectual activity things had reached a stage of advanced orderliness. Certain overexcited charlies were signing on for three years' graft at subjects for which they were inadequately prepared. Little of what I learned at the hands of Caerleon's pedagogues stood me in good stead for the years ahead. The idea was to enthuse us with a love of learning that would last until our retirement presentation. Thus charged with missionary zeal, we would flow like worker ants out into the shires to prepare oncoming generations for the twenty-first century. You studied two main subjects, or one main with two subsidiaries. I chose the latter, plumping for Religious Education and English. Meanwhile my parents had retired to the hills whence they had come, a small army of lecturers were trading notes about this year's intake, and enterprising cooks were dreaming up yet more companion dishes for the overworked French fry.

Most students were straight out of sixth form. Girls outnumbered boys, or appeared to; perhaps it was just that I noticed them more. The boys were a pretty uninspiring bunch, with the emphasis on uninspiring rather than pretty. A surprising number had cauliflower ears and pug noses. Ally this to a heavy gait, a thick neck, and fingers like pork sausages, and the conclusion was inescapable. Rugby players. I had been delivered from the place which patched them up to the place which geed them up. So long as the pastime was non-obligatory I would not mind.

The next ploy was to advance and be recognised at the right speed and by the right people, if there were any. Drama students had, like me, a lightness of tone and a bad complexion (these were pre-jogging days when smoking was *de rigueur,* though I never indulged in the noxious weed myself). Few had any experience of theatre beyond being taken to see *Mother Goose* as a child. Sybil Hollingdrake, the woman who had enlisted me on her course, had read English at Bristol and had an infectious fervour for the subject. Florrie Watts, her colleague, was equally hefty, equally spinsterish, and Jewish to boot. Frank Platts proceeded by fits and starts and let off whooshes of enthusiastic utterance as the spirit moved him. He was not unlikeable, such unease as existed being generated by the presumption that he was always right. When at full stretch, giving his own inimitable slant on Joe Orton or August Strindberg, there was no stopping him. Alan Storey, the librarian and our fourth lecturer, was a model of worldly sardonicism and knowing introspection.

In no time leaders began to emerge from the pack, or maybe they were just jokers. Foremost were Mike Hayward and Jean Greenhalgh. Now Mike and Jean *had* something, that *je ne sais quoi* which allows you to know it when you see it yet not to analyse it. Had they been at RADA it might have been called magic, the old Spencer Tracy-Katharine Hepburn chemistry, the Richard Burton-Elizabeth Taylor rapport of around 1962. Not that they were in love - no, nothing so corny. They had *style*. The pity was the size of their stage. They were performing in Toytown. In the real world they might have triumphed. But then every tuppenny ha'penny tinpot college of education in the country had its Mikes and Jeans. Most never made the grade, though at that moment, suffused as these two were by the bloom of youth, anything seemed possible.

The union president and vice-president were Jeff Mudford and Pat Jones. During my second year they were David Jeremiah and Anita Griffiths. Whatever happened to these stalwarts? Their reigns were brief, as were their officials', individuals responsible for everything from overseeing Food and Laundry to expressing solidarity with the Sandinistas of Nicaragua. This mock government, a toothless tiger, encountered little interference from the real administrators. It would wander onto the stage before a crowded auditorium, occupy a line of chairs, and look self-important. There was, after all, business to discuss. The front row of the audience would consist of barracking, wind-breaking backs and forwards. Soon Jeff, or David, would clear his throat.

"Could I have your attention please." The request generally provoked ribaldry and intemperate laughter from the first fifteen. "This evening's meeting...."

There would be more falling about. Mind you, one president in particular would have made a statue split its sides. Was there a more inept spokesman in Christendom, a less grammatical ad-libber? His spoonerisms and malapropisms were inspired, though by what dubious agency we never found out. Language was forever dropping its trousers at his command and the spectators loved it, some laughing with him, most at him. To cobble together a semblance of constitutional progress following his first catastrophic pronouncements was extremely difficult. It says much for the power of the human mind that something could usually be salvaged. The meetings came not so much to an orderly as to a dry conclusion: internal hydrostats clicked on and the muscle-bound oiks drifted off towards the local pubs. Their progress was down to such a fine art that volition no longer played a part. Having perfected the means of staggering back to their rooms on autopilot, they could, stone-cold sober, accomplish the feat in reverse. Thus they moved, zombie-like, to the village. Mary Wollstonecraft Shelley could hardly have created a more chilling spectacle, nor any Haitian peasant, versed in voodoo, have witnessed one. Once they had gone the heart went out of the meeting. Jeff, or David, would cruise on perfunctorily, speaking increasingly to the backs of heads and the dinning of chairs. The student council were still in place, as imperturbable as Meissen toby jugs. Their audience had dwindled to wets, lonely hearts, and the staff-room activists of tomorrow.

What, you might ask, were these taverns like: decorous alehouses with old-timers chatting peaceably in corners? Quaint snugs where quoits and shove-halfpenny were the rule? Chapels of indulgence with oaken beer-pulls and settles? I never actually found out because, once inside, you could not see beyond the crush of bodies and the density of tobacco fumes. The perceived noise decibels were akin to standing on a Stanwell rooftop as a DC-8 retracted its undercarriage seemingly inches above you. As long ago as the 4th century BC, Aristippus of Cyrene advocated the pleasure principle as the supreme bench mark of living. Were these propinquitous drinkers his heirs they might have had the right idea yet they would have had the wrong way of expressing it. The sole compensation lay in the possibility of frottage, depending where your hands were immobilised. If they were at chest height, then with luck you might be juxtaposed against a female of the species, preferably with large bristols. You had short odds of lodging your tankard in her cleavage. If nothing transpired, at least it was still possible for lips to reach froth. The really hopeful kept their lager at crotch height, anticipating a tactile bonanza. If unsuccessful they would go thirsty, or wet themselves trying to hoist the glass past their navel. It was a unique, bizarre way of spending the evening, from which you emerged like a kipper, dull-eyed and smoked.

You did not *have* to go pub-crawling. You could curl up

with a book, say Maria Montessori's *The Secret of Childhood* (1936) or A.S. Neill's *That Dreadful School* of the following year. You could. But you did not. You were more absorbed with yourself and others than with educational theory. The language which most interested you was body. Hardly anyone had scored, apart from between H-shaped posts; and one's petting quotient was nothing to write home about, not that one would have written home about it had it been. No, we were untried in the intricacies of intimacy. Soon the world would mourn the passing of Gregory Pincus, Father of the Pill. While Signorina Montessori was worrying her head about childhood's secret, Pincus published his tome *The Eggs of Mammals*. The next three decades saw him develop a fool-proof contraceptive, using Caribbean women as guinea pigs. At the time of his death he was perfecting the morning-after prophylactic. There was no rush. We did not need it yet. However, soon we would be waylaid by the Rolling Stones' *Let's Spend The Night Together* so perhaps mothers were right to be concerned. What would happen to Daphne's career if she got pregnant? It hardly bore thinking about. Her mythical namesake had the good fortune to turn into a laurel tree when pursued by a randy Apollo; a modern miss would have no such luck. The Rolling Stones were not solely to blame; the start of the sixties had Marilyn Monroe and Yves Montand suggesting *Let's Make Love*, while nearer home we thrilled to saucy Barbara Windsor's barely concealed boobs in *Carry On* films. I had not fondly touched a female in three years.

For reasons that escape me, three other boys and four girls piled into a scruffy Bedford van and crossed the original Severn Bridge considerably quicker than Her Majesty had when opening it two months earlier. We were bound for romantic old Bristol, old because it was a Royal Borough before the Norman Conquest, romantic because things were looking up. One of our number - Jane Sheppard - had caught my eye.

Being improvident and impecunious, we had not arranged sleeping accommodation, so after several hours of cavorting feyly in cobbled alleyways and venerable thoroughfares, with frequent entry into characterful bars, we arrived at Temple Meads railway station as the witching hour approached. Under the waiting room's bright lights we waited brightly, though for what we could not say. Somehow I found myself fighting tiredness with wit and sparkle. She did likewise. She had a svelte body, a certain wayward artiness, and a winsome Wiltshire accent, moved with leonine grace, and should have featured in a shampoo commercial gliding through fields of rape. Her father was a college lecturer in Bath, she had a younger sister named Judy, and the family lived at Shaw near Melksham. She might as well have been Jasmine from Harrogate, or Kate from Tunbridge Wells, or.... The possibilities were endless, unless one is a fatalist. As we were mutually focusing to the exclusion of everyone else in the universe so were a zillion other nascent lovers from Pyongyang to Putney. Such affection was not entirely platonic. I still wanted to visit that town between the thighs called Maidenhead, surely Britain's sexiest place name.

Enter the concept of the dormitory, the single-sex hall of residence, the eleven p.m. curfew. This was strictly enforced by a shrewish spoilsport who patrolled with a bunch of keys precisely on the hour; a Swiss stationmaster could not have been more unnervingly punctual. Nearby, writhing upright couples attempted to ram tongues down throats or embroil fingers within the tortuous elasticity of undergarments. The shadows ached with asthmatics minus their inhalers. The enforced lameness of a 'Good night' ensued, and rubescent maidens disappeared reluctantly indoors. Each disgruntled beau shuffled off as best he could, given that his briefs contained a torpedo whose target-finder was in an advanced state of readiness. The divine restitution of the weekend was therefore avidly awaited. Then you penetrated the penetralia of these forbidding hostels, bearing a jar of coffee, a few flowers, and the Small Faces' first LP. Their number one UK single *All*

Or Nothing more or less summed up our requirements. That most of us got Nothing made the chance of getting All appear the more glorious. Meanwhile my inamorata and I were proceeding chastely, with only occasional fully clothed genital apposition to appease Eros. Would consummation come, and if so when and where would the breakthrough occur? I toyed with the idea of blurting out my need for a packet of vulcanised-rubber thingummies in Boots but had yet to venture inside. That the Egyptian Ebers papyrus of 1,500 BC had right little goers along the Nile Valley screwing merrily against a vaginal plug of lint and honey served only to heighten my disconsolation. Thomas Hardy's gripe - *After two thousand years of mass / We've got as far as poison-gas* - was as nothing compared with mine: *After three thousand years of protection / We still can't deal with a student's erection.* So we talked, and professed undying love, and sojourned at each other's home. Misty rural walks remain in the mind, visits to Lacock and Norton St Philip, easy conversing against a very English background - like the Duke and Duchess of York honeymooning in April 1923 (photographs show relaxed strollers a good yard apart, as if it was considered indecorous even for newly-weds to link fingers in front of a lens).

I suppose lust finally burst the balloon. In an earlier age it might have been easier to have a pure relationship of the mind, like two baboons discussing Frege. As it was we were examples of *Homo sapiens* hunched, with simian intensity, over our sickening libidos without the wherewithal or nerve to slake our passion. This was the era of Joseph Losey's *Accident*, a film whose domestic civilities were charged with tempestuous undercurrents as the sky suffused purple and a few intemperate raindrops spattered your face. Ennui. Bumble-bees rolling their little fatnesses against tremendous anthers and stigmas, drunk with summer. Streams, full of themselves, sliding between mossy banks. Cows hardly raising their heads from intoxicating grasses, a superabundance of lushness. The waters of Babylon were flowing, as through *Belshaz-*

zar's *Feast*, and like that hapless king I was devouring the fruits of my ineptitude while the writing mysteriously appeared on the wall. I needed no Daniel to interpret its foreboding. As in the choral symphony, the atmosphere was electric, a mingling of bloodthirsty exultation and barbaric splendour. The fact that little was said rendered the drama properly Pinteresque. When we finally snapped, Armageddon raged, but all I had to show for it was a hairgrip and a cup of cold cappuccino.

She had the elegance of a Saluki. I had the plainness of a Rottweiler. Her antecedents hunted gazelle in the deserts of Araby. Mine mustered cattle on a Bavarian smallholding. A plighted troth was not to be had, which in a way was just as well, for had it been I would not have played the field with such alacrity in the years to come. For some weeks, though, I traipsed about in a miasma of self-pity which was exacerbated when she happened upon a replacement and I did not. Being of a poetic turn of mind, I almost relished my discomfiture. Life became a sad autumnal sunset, smeared with Pre-Raphaelite colours and impregnated with Tennysonian angst. Indeed, had it not been at Caerleon's Hanbury Arms that the bard had written, around 1833, 'The Lady of Shallot'. And was it not the prerogative of the spring onion to evoke crocodile tears.

Meanwhile second-rate savants were boning up on didactics with deadly seriousness. Somewhere textbook pupils were waiting to be taught textbook lessons. Soon we would be exposed to teaching practices among pint pots into whom we would attempt to pour quarts of knowledge. The greatest folly of young adults is their belief that they can change the world. In the vast majority of cases the world changes them. Most compromise their ideals, many become disillusioned, some crack up, a few are driven to ending it all. Noisy kids come and go, leapfrogging browbeaten staff and consigning ink pellets hither and thither with abandon.

How did I fit into this? Jokily. I never took the place

seriously. Anyone who did must have been touched. Had I been lined up for Greats it might have been different. Had my consciousness been immersed in Homeric Archaeology and Comparative Philology, Plato's *Republic* and Aristotle's *Nicomachean Ethics*, fair dinkum, sport. It was not. You would find more scholarship on a shithouse wall than here in Philistia, but this was grist to my mill. Erudition you could get from a book. I hankered after social intercourse and that was pursued using an entirely different set of values.

Our first public performance was Bertolt Brecht's last play *The Caucasian Chalk Circle*. It was chosen primarily because of its large cast. There would have been little point in staging, say, Beckett's minimalist *Happy Days* except to massage the egos of Mike and Jean. No, we needed a blockbuster, a Hyde Park Corner of commotion. It ran for three nights, and the star of the show - as the rascally judge Adzak - turned out to be Bill Hancox, Tackle Officer of the Caving Club.

One had to admit that thespians had the most legitimate fun. Play-acting is as pleasurable for twenty-year-olds as for five-year-olds. The only merriment which could compete was illegitimate and indulged in largely by natives of the male hostel who banded together according to tribal origin: the Brazilian rainforest, the New Guinea Highlands, the Rhondda Valley. Pronunciation was all-important. When the Beach Boys sang *Help Me Rhonda* they were not seeking assistance from mean little terraced back-to-backs and intimidatory winding gear. Two d s and an a was enunciated as in *Ron, the bath's overflowing*. Which is peculiarly apt, since a near-o'erflowing bath constituted the trademark of certain valley lads. Most initiation ceremonies have a mystic, semi-religious nature; those conducted by the rugby boys were not thus ennobled. Essentially they consisted of loutish horse-play akin to post-match changing-room foolery. This included breaking down someone's door and dragging him off to be debagged, given a pubic shave with a blunt razor, and tossed into a bath of cold water enlivened with cocoa powder, dog-ends, and urine. Protesters were considered unmanly. Whinging was for milksops. If you could emerge like Al Jolson with sore bollocks and beam charitably at your assailants you were a man, my son. I preferred to remain blissfully puerile. To that end I barricaded myself in with a chest of drawers every night for two years. More than once bibulous raiding-parties sought access, giving up when a dislocated shoulder seemed imminent. Had there been no stout impediment the door would have yielded in seconds. The reason every such entrance was not permanently smashed was that marauders could patch things up convincingly next morning, being by and large Metalwork and Woodwork hulks. All male residents could fall prey to this: fellow Celts from excessive exuberance, the English from a hostility born of Llywelyn ap Gruffydd's defeat by Edward I in 1282. Although a blunt razor had little chance of accidentally castrating the victim, the experience could put him off cocoa for life.

Roger Griffiths, an ex-Monmouth School colleague, had preceded me into Caerleon by a year. His dislike of these conceited dunderheads matched mine exactly, yet he trusted more to native cunning than to makeshift defences. When a posse attempted to initiate him he hurriedly locked his door against them and leapt from his second-floor window onto a drainpipe, shinned down, and sprawled on the pavement. In crashed the hearties, only to find the sash raised and their quarry lying fifty feet below. The toughs hid in their rooms until nightfall, sick with fear and immersed in Nonconformist prayer. They were as distraught to find him resurrected behind a plate of chips in the cafeteria that evening as they had been to survey his corpse hours before. He was never bothered thereafter.

In my last year he and I accomplished a sting. It was Rag Week and we organised a raid on Cardiff College of Education. Intent on mayhem, six of us trundled down to the capital at midnight. Breaking in was a cinch. We ransacked the kitchen, emptied flour around the hall, and generally strove to make Caerleon unpopular. Next day heated telephone calls began arriving. The atmosphere having been properly soured, the time was right for 'retaliation'. A few nights later, when our rugged beauties were abed in their usual stupor, he and I and two fetching second-year girls crept along their corridor, removed light bulbs, plugged locks with putty, chalked *Cardiff for Ever* all over the place, and turned on the fire hydrants. We retired to a safe distance down the drive, shivering with chill and excitement beneath the astonished stars. For a while nothing happened. Then windows lit up one by one. Soon every bedroom was ablaze with consternation as waterlogged residents grappled with recalcitrant doors; those that did open led onto flooded passageways with inoperable lights. Roger and I fled to his flat off St Vincent Road, Newport while our plucky female assistants returned to their hostel which they entered by fair means or foul.

Roger was one of the most engagingly reckless characters I had ever met. On Thursday 20th May 1965, following a school trip to see *Oliver!* at the Duke of York's Theatre in London, he had failed to return to Victoria Coach Station for the homeward journey. Our senior master, Mr. H.E. Phillips, had paced up and down the gangway demanding "Where *is* the boy?" as if seats and skylight could provide an answer. It transpired he had met a journalist in a bar, dined with him, and slept at his Ilford flat. The rest of us returned to exasperated parents in Monmouth around dawn. The following week Roger entered our study red-eyed and shaking, having been suspended by the headmaster, Mr. R.F. Glover.

This aberration prefigured one five years later when he and I bombed off to Bristol in his van ostensibly to make whoopee. Oddly, the vehicle was behaving like a buffeted hovercraft, aquaplaning wildly despite the dryness of the road. A check on the forecourt of Larkfield Garage, Chepstow showed the pressure in two of the tyres was greatly more than it should have been. It was his first trip in the banger and beforehand he had simply stamped on the foot pump until his leg tired, hoping this constituted sufficient attention. At our destination we drifted aimlessly like Jon Voigt and Dustin Hoffman, stars of the recently released *Midnight Cowboy* though without their panache. Unsurprisingly, we did not find ourselves pursued by hordes of slavering nymphos. We called it a day at a Fairfax Street snack bar, both trying to charm the same faintly amused young woman. Soon he gave up and went for a walk. Eventually she gave up and went home. Finally I gave up visions of happy hustling and wandered back to the van. It had disappeared. Being virtually broke, I tramped off to St. James's Parade, hard by the Bus Station, and tried sleeping on a park bench. Fat chance. The shivers arrived; the metabolism sagged; numbness set in. There was nothing for it other than to await the mercies of dawn. When it came I hitched to the A449 and three hours later arrived at Roger's farm. He was playfully roughing up his dog on the lawn. I could have flattened him. Such were his winning ways and my willing gullibility that I told him off and left it at that. Over the years I had been entertained by him greatly more than I had been inconvenienced by him so the occasional shortcoming was forgivable. Ultimately, he owed me nothing and I owed him nothing; we were out for ourselves, neither of us taking life seriously, sensing all the while this unencumbered light-mindedness would not last. Perhaps such breeziness is the principal freedom of the young.

Already my youth had been knocked awry. Someone I had regarded as a childhood sweetheart had married on Saturday 1st April 1967, too late in the day for it to register as a practical joke. Strangely, I felt neither elation nor despair. I did not care about her wedding night, her unrobed splendour crossing the room towards another's arms, the freshness of her face against the hotel pillow. My heart was frozen. While the congregation sang *Lead us, heavenly Father, lead us o'er the world's tempestuous sea* I was landlocked within the medieval coolness of Penallt Old Church. Its graveyard's skeletal couples had once been just as enraptured as these two. Was my stance sour grapes? Was it an armour against the seepage of emotion? Or was it that *Belle de Jour*, Luis Buñuel's disconcerting masterpiece about womanly concupiscence, had recently sent me reeling from the cinema in a state of nervous exhaustion? From now on wives would never seem quite so safely unimaginative, so hidebound by convention, so tied to stultifying routine. Although these two were tying the knot, Engelbert Humperdinck was pleading *Release Me* at the summit of the pop charts. Meanwhile, twenty-year-old male virgins were an embarrassment, to themselves and to others. I was worrying about which Eve would accompany me through Eden with the intensity of Adam perusing *Playboy*.

I required a double life, with college flappers *and* homespun cuties. This meant tweaking my image. Chekhov, Shakespeare, Shaw, and Strindberg had sported beards. As a stagy satyr I needed one too. It conferred mystique and authority worlds away from mud-besmirched line-outs and scrums. I wore a jacket and tie while others staggered back from The Bull or The Drovers Arms in vomit-stained jeans. I vowed never again to be caught out by gaucheness in matters of the bedroom. My eyes narrowed and my brain went into overdrive. I would either lose my cherry before coming of age or start a monastery on Kerguelen.

When the academic year ended, my parents took me to Coleford in the Forest of Dean. Stepping off a coach in the town centre were zwei jolly Fräuleins who were to stay with us for a fortnight; then I was to stay with eine jolly deutsch family, thereby fostering international détente. One was a plump brunette, daughter of a mining academy official; the other was a slim blonde, daughter of a tiler. This information was deemed relevant so that we could talk in terms of mining or tiling if all else failed. The group of which these two were a part spent its first night in Britain at the YMCA in Bulstrode Street, Westminster. They visited Windsor Castle en route to

Gloucestershire, where a party was laid on for them. Stratford-upon-Avon, Coventry Cathedral, and Braceland Farm were on the itinerary. Braceland Farm? This was a base convenient for abseiling and canoeing amid attractive scenery. Instead of Clint Eastwood and Richard Burton machine-gunning squads of Germans in *Where Eagles Dare* we stood a fair chance of losing a few of them to outdoor pursuits. Failing that we would bore them to death with Kultur: a square dance at the local secondary school, and talks by local worthies on English Music, Forest History, and Modes & Manners. To leaven the dough, further trips were planned: rubbernecking in Bath and Cardiff, and swimming at Ross-on-Wye and Porthcawl. When we visited their country between Thursday 3rd and Friday 18th August it would be my first time abroad. Twenty years old and yet to leave Blighty! I was not the only one; few contemporaries had left it either. The age of routine continental travel was just beginning. This was the threshold of a new era: that of the first heart transplant, the decriminalisation of homosexuality in Britain, and Francis Chichester yachting solo around the world. Anything was possible. Within two years they might even land on the moon!

Thus on the lookout for gay sailors with chest scars, I fraternised freely with our Aryan guests. On their first day with us the Latey Commission advocated that eighteen should be the age of majority. I was well beyond it, and the busty brunette (almost nineteen, the oldest in the group) was more woman than girl, so what were we waiting for? Within a week I had managed to get her alone in the front room. Her blonde companion and my parents were out for the evening. She had a headache so I was detailed to stay and look after her. A hot little baggage, more Mediterranean than north European, she sat tucked up on the sofa bed wearing a baby-doll nightie. She was self-consciously alluring, probably a prickteaser, yet really rather sweet. In patient English I asked if she had done it with anyone. With venerable deliberation she ran her fingers through her hair, looked at what - had we been outside -

would have been far clouds, and sighed pneumatically. Pumpkin breasts rose and fell.

"Ja," she answered. "I haf."

"With whom?" I enquired, by turns crestfallen and elated.

"My boyfriend I am thinking. We are lovers this once."

"And - er - what was it like?"

She considered, as if inspecting a hand of cards. Then the revelation burst forth. "Wunderbar! I am enjoying it greatly. It eeza moss beautifool theeng ever."

By now I was drooling like a Pavlovian pooch and breathing fast. "Would you c-care to repeat the experience?" She nodded brightly. "How about this very minute?" I had said it! Would she slap my face; worse, tell my parents? I was ready to blurt out a pathetic 'Sorry' when she smiled a little sadly.

"Ah - deeer Paul, how I like you." She brushed my cheek with her hand. Instantly I fumbled for my zip, brain clouding over and loins quivering with electricity. "Ah - no." What was that? "No. You are too nice."

"I'm not, I swear it. I'm just like your boyfriend back home; not a bit nice. You'll see. Just give me a chance. You'll love it."

"Ah, no. We remain platonisch friends." Stuff Plato. He always managed to foul things up.

"I swear - I love you - I think you're very wunderbar too."

She shook her head sagely and wordlessly pulled down the front of her nightdress. Two magnificent breasts appeared in their pristine entirety, nipples balanced like pfennigs. I kissed them reverently, as if they were the Pope's feet, and they were put away again.

The other German girls that summer were haltingly bilingual flaxen-haired maidens who were bourgeois rather than bohemian, despite Bohemia being nearer to their back door than to mine. Their fathers doubtless cruised around in

BMWs and Mercedes-Benzes. One day their husbands would be clean-cut industrialists, younger versions of their fathers. Their daughters would resemble these Fräuleins and in turn marry 21st-century industrialists who would be clones of *their* fathers. When accompanying the party to their stylish homes jaundice properly set in. How did the Forest of Dean have the nerve to twin itself, however loosely, with the Harz Mountains? Apart from a no-man's-land of barbed wire and booby traps between the Democratic and Federal Republics, this gentle upland area was magnificent. Bad Harzburg, Braunlage, and Goslar were truly impressive. In comparison, Cinderford, Coleford, and Lydney were depressingly drab.

I stayed with Michael, whose parents ran a bookshop in the town of Clausthal-Zellerfeld. The extent of my linguistic ability was *Ja, Nein, Bitte, Danke, Guten Morgen, Auf Wiedersehen* and, of course, *Wunderbar*. On my return I would have mastered *Wo ist die Toilette, Sprechen Sie englisch* and *Prosit* and would even be proud of the fact. Our hosts pointed out the needful in broken English and we nodded energetically: *Ja, ja, ja, ja, ja*. That the gibbering continued but for a brief span was its sole redeeming feature. By the time their forbearance wore thin we would be saying *Auf Wiedersehen* and promising to write. Until then we had some living to do. Berlin.

Our coach slipped along the open road and we dozed. All of a sudden it halted. Helmstedt Checkpoint. Were we to be frisked? The guards' faces were impassive. Nothing To Declare. Eventually we restarted our journey. A hundred-and-fifty more kilometres. When we finally arrived we were among 'friends'. After settling in at our hotel we went to a nightclub. No trip to this city would be complete without such a visit. My current handbook mentions Big Eden and Rajneesh Disco, both on Kurfürstendamm, and the Buccaneer on Rankestrasse. It does not list our destination that evening: the Riverboat. My memory is of a large building whose throbbing top floor was jammed with revellers, many quite alarmingly pretty. Clearly no amount of commie cant was going to stop these youngsters enjoying themselves.

We saw the ghost of Jesse Owens powering around the Olympic Stadium. Strange: he still had thirteen years to live. The place was empty, yet echoes of Leni Reifenstahl's *Olympische Spiele* rang in our ears. Then there was the Brandenburg Gate surmounted by a winged statue and four-horse chariot. This bronze quadriga of Nike and her team seemed almost alive. It embodied a nation's spirit, binoculars and tripwires notwithstanding. The metropolis appeared riven by schizophrenia into a hothouse of past decadence and present uncertainty. There was nothing for it other than to fork your Black Forest gâteau and ponder the inadequacy of human wishes. We visited the Kaiser Wilhelm Memorial Church, the 453-foot-tall Radio Tower, the *Schandmauer* or 'wall of shame' breached for us at Checkpoint Charley, the vast Tiergarten, and the Wannsee - Berlin's biggest lake - where for the only time in my life I fancied the men as much as the women. Strolling along the sand were Adonises with skin every bit as golden; emerging from the water were Adonises with eyes every bit as blue.

Soon we had to return across the plain with its woods and scattered homesteads, along the four-lane concrete highway to what we naïvely called Freedom and to the Volkspolizei or 'People's police' - Vopos for short - who wheeled mirrors beneath your vehicle to find out if anyone was hidden there. I imagined the fugitive, crucified against the chassis and deafened by tyre roar, and hoped he'd get free, yet knew the Vopos would always position a reflecting trolley under his nose after a hundred miles of hell and smile victoriously. It was fun to replicate President Kennedy's words of four years before - 'Ich bin ein Berliner' - though it did not mean much as we were hightailing it away from the city as fast as our wheels could carry us.

Back in the Harz Mountains, Ingrid introduced me to her boyfriend. As with Berlin, I might never glimpse her beautiful secrets again. This guy would. He would experience repeatedly what I had closely missed: being inside the resplendent Pullman of her body, which had gathered speed away from me a week or so earlier. I comforted myself with the realisation that there would be other trains to catch. It was simply a matter of being on the right platform at the right time, though occasionally I doubted if I was even at the right station.

It was the summer of the Beatles' *All You Need Is Love* and Scott McKenzie's *San Francisco*. The exhortation was to wear flowers in your hair. Marianne wore some in hers and bought *Sergeant Pepper's Lonely Hearts Club Band*. Christa, with the flaming red locks, needed no floral adornment. Birgit, who lived with her grandparents, had the longest tresses of all. Then there was Ulrike, a probation officer's daughter, who was to write to me for two years. She said she wanted to be a great lover. The fact that she had yet to notch up a single conquest did not deter her. She was to send me postcards from around Europe. Klimt's *Der Kuß* suited her well, as did Manet's *Blumen in Kristallvase* and Renoir's *Auf der Terrasse*. Then there was Nolde's *Zinnien und Lilien*. We had a right little thing going, she sending me arty cards, I sending her soppy letters concocted from phrasebook German and kindergarten English. The replies would come, often in green ink. *What are you doing? Are you still writing poems? You did never wrote one for me. (I'm sad about)* Why have I kept them? They are oddly touching, their innocent scrawl extending page after page to a heart beside her name. *Now with curlers in my hair (I look awful). Didn't you got my letter? Are you doing German? Please do, I would like to hear some of you.*

She was born on 8th August 1952 and was seventeen when I last saw her - in the Wye Valley. She was staying at The Priory, Llandogo, courtesy of The Holiday Fellowship. I drove the three miles to meet her and brought her home for tea. It was Monday 21st July 1969. As we sipped decorously from the best china, our eyes were not for each other. Affection was upstaged by Americans steering a lunar module above the Sea of Tranquillity. The computer was overloaded and the human race was holding its breath. Our cups hovered about our lips as we watched the monochrome pictures flicker before us. Although it had happened at 3.56 a.m. British Standard Time, now was the hour that millions of fellow countrymen were following the descent of the intrepid astronauts.

That summer's activities had started for me on Friday 12th May. Alan Williams and I were Team 60 in the College Rag Week Hitching Race. Which twosome would manage to boomerang themselves the greatest distance from Caerleon's Goldcroft Inn by 6.00 p.m. on the 14th? A stipulation was that public transport should be avoided unless essential. By midnight we were stranded near Whitchurch, Shropshire, shivery, hungry, and facing a long walk. It took until dawn to reach Tarporley. Bickley Moss damply came and went as did Ridley Green. None of the few motorists who passed was keen to pluck bedraggled strangers from beside the A49. It was wretched marching through darkness in the middle of nowhere. Near Bunbury Heath a van rescued us and we breakfasted at a Warrington transport café. The next step was to read cab doors in the car park. One said Perth. We waited keenly for the driver to appear. Forty minutes elapsed. He was nowhere to be seen. I re-entered the building. Alan checked the washroom. Half a dozen blokes were eating. I lurked uneasily. Alan mooched around with even less grace. He was a gangling lad, bespectacled and prone to blushing. The sight of him ogling beefy itinerants in the toilets was definitely suspect and he incurred several menacing glances. Where was our knight of the road? Just then a head appeared near the steering wheel, followed by a hand rubbing sleepy eyes. Stiff from his nap along the front seat, he stretched and sat up, gunning the engine. We ran over, hammered his door, and asked for that special lift. He mumbled something in Lallans which did not sound unfriendly so we climbed aboard.

For hours we travelled north, lulled by the engine.

None of us spoke much. Scores of miles passed, the warm cab granting us uncomfortable but much-needed slumber. No radio blared, and the road was a mesmerist's watch. Wigan, Preston, Garstang, Lancaster, Kendal, Penrith, Carlisle, Langholm, Hawick, Selkirk, *Edinburgh*. Although he had planned to stop there awhile, he went out of his way to set us up for the next leg of the journey. The Forth Bridge reared like a humpback whale. Broadly parallel was the Rail Bridge, its unseen painters never-endingly applying red oxide, and Robert Donat and Madeleine Carroll hurrying across it in the film *The 39 Steps*. We called it a day at the village of Coupar Angus. Dreams of reaching John o'Groats faded. What if, after all this bedlessness and effort, others had beaten us to the Highlands and beyond? It hardly bore thinking about. A bobby stamped our docket with proof of arrival and we turned tail for home. Dog-tired, we caught the Perth-to-Sterling bus and the Carlisle train, off which we staggered at 4.00 a.m. We virtually crawled into the local hospital, gasping for coffee or another stimulant. A benevolent staff nurse brewed a pot of tea and provided a few biscuits. We wanted to stay for at least ten hours of unbroken bed-rest. She shook her head ruefully and we were on our way again.

I cannot remember getting down through England. All I know is we arrived at Hereford late on Sunday. Alan continued alone. I telephoned my parents, who were unwilling to come the twenty miles from home to pick me up. Consequently I trudged off to the police station and begged to be locked up for the night. They refused, until I told them my half-brother Douglas was an officer in the county. They knew him and this made them relent. I was given a blanket and a spartan cell. Nonetheless I slept soundly. Later I was to discover we had gone the greatest distance and would be the proud recipients of £1. When I got back to Caerleon I was duly presented with my share: a grubby ten-bob note.

Would this taxing experience put me off hitching for ever? Not a bit of it. On Monday 3rd July 1967 Roger Griffiths and I made for a metropolis whose streets were paved not just with gold but with every hue in the rainbow. Two days earlier the BBC had started colour broadcasts, thereby extending the moment's heady polychromatism. Riotous abandon blossomed. We did not even bother to fix stamps to our postcards: 3d was far too much when euphoria was free. To paraphrase Wordsworth, bliss it was in those days to be alive, but to be young was very heaven! London was the centre of the known universe, and Piccadilly Circus effectively the centre of London. At its core stood Eros, aiming an arrow at the hearts of all for whom love was a genuine possibility. This angel of Christian charity (and the Freudian force which promoted uninhibited indulgence) rendered us impassive and exhilarated for hours on end.

The Swinging London myth (most inhabitants worked as feverishly as ever, racy leisureliness applying mostly to teenagers and tourists) commanded our awe and admiration as if it were more real than reality. We wandered up and down Carnaby Street declaring *Man, the whole scene is a gas!* We found boutiques with weird and wonderful names like Granny Takes a Trip and Kleptomania and counted our coppers in an attempt to afford lunch at The Chelsea Kitchen (not difficult: two courses plus a carafe of wine cost 10s). The quintessentially hip places were beyond our reach: Annabel's in Berkeley Square, Dolly's in Jermyn Street, Samantha's in Burlington Street, and the Beatle-backed discotheque for incognito jet-setters, Sibylla's in Swallow Street. Adopting the principle that for every beautiful person at an exclusive nightspot twenty others roamed freely, we told ourselves that outside was the in-place and that many inside places were on the way out. Or, to quote John Lennon, *Your inside is out and your outside is in.* Consciousness became a Möbius strip with no inside or outside, simply a tape which went round forever. It was the darkened glass of a pop idol's limo where you glimpsed his face, or was it your own? Life was a semipermeable membrane which allowed a constant influx and outflux of ideas. Whoever could be a sober teacher after this?

We spent our first night in Regent's Park, seeking sleep beneath an orange sky and against the city's incessant presence. I recall crawling under an azalea bush near Queen Mary's Gardens, only to disturb a snoozing Frenchman. After a heartfelt *sacrebleu!* he turned over and resumed his shut-eye. Next day we trekked in a transfluvial direction, slaking our thirst on nicked pintas. It was hot and fumy. Too much was happening, quite unlike in Monmouthshire. The ground was hard and everything cost something. An answer, we decided with louche bravado, was to hit the south coast and score. No sweat. Unfortunately there was rather a lot. Morden, the most southerly Underground station, promised sweet release. When we arrived there were no meadows and cowslips as fondly imagined, just more of the same. Bustling pavements. Oppressive warmth. Fuggy air.

When we finally reached Brighton we were bushed. Hardy travellers have returned from the Hindu Kush bronzed and resilient after subsisting on iron rations. They have encountered fiercely brave Pathan tribesmen, endured choking dust and blistering heat, undergone nights when the mercury sank past zero, and struggled up 60° slopes burdened with bulky backpacks and debilitating diarrhoea. We, by contrast, were still in the Home Counties. Stupidly we felt we were breaking new ground and being toweringly daring, when all around us perfectly ordinary people were doing perfectly ordinary things. We were exploring the jungle of our own fantasies, using the machete of expectation to hack towards whatever constituted that personal El Dorado. Not fabulous trinkets and overflowing gem-boxes, but a pint, a pork pie, and a pretty girl.

A Portslade resident took us to meet his family, who, undeterred by our unkempt appearance, gave us a meal in their trim detached house. Later he showed us round in a glistening saloon with a wooden dashboard and leather seats.

Brighton hove into view. He set us down beside the elegant cast-iron columns of Madeira Drive where he said the annual Veteran Car Rally finished. Then his own car bore him into the realms of memory, leaving us excited and apprehensive on the pavement.

The resort had long been renowned for raffishness. A painting by Whistler in the Royal Pavilion - *The Prince Regent Awakening the Spirit of Brighton* - showed a near-nude lifting a sleeping girl's veil. As we gazed about us it was clear that many of the promenading females were exceedingly attractive. Some looked Scandinavian. *Yeah, man,* we were told by a switched-on youth in peacock finery, *the place is an arable farm. Loads of Swedes.* Dusk swathed these enchantresses; cooking smells filled the air; pop music sounded from intriguing doorways and raised windows. The rustle of silk, the thwack of sandals, the sight of Kurdish shepherd bags slung from divinely feminine shoulders, the scent of illegal substances: this could have removed any sceptic's doubt as to the existence of heaven. And if there were houris in the afterlife I would have bet a packet of poppy seeds none wore a crisscross nonslip longline bra. Furthermore, Paradise *had* to be diaphanous.

For the princely sum of 2/- you could enter the Pop In Beat Club, which we did. Loud, dark, vital, it heaved with bodies exuding compelling odours of animal sexuality. We sheepishly chatted up the same bird, a Vietnamese student resident in Paris. Swarthy, doe-eyed, graceful of movement and gentle of manner, she was many a man's dream-made-flesh. Her features hinted at a quiet deep intelligence; she had long black hair; and the curve of her spine was a Grieg glissando, something in A flat (these four words being what we wanted). Unfortunately she spoke hardly a word of English.

"Meal, yes?" She nodded. We were starving and she appeared to be peckish. We happened upon a Chinese restaurant, stumbled in tiredly, and perused the menu.

"I'll have everything," quipped Roger.

She became perplexed. "You eat all?"

He reassured her. "No, no - joke."

She frowned. "What is joke?" She peered at the bill of fare in the indifferent light. "Me joke too? Good food?"

Roger swore under his breath. "She's all yours," he conceded.

"No food called joke," I explained. "We eat this - or this - or this. You too?"

"Me too."

"Which?" asked Roger.

"Yes," she smiled with satisfaction, lacing her fingers on her lap. He exhaled as if with his last breath and rolled his eyes towards the decorative lanterns.

After forty minutes of eating and drinking and trying to converse in Franglais we bad our companion *au revoir* and walked off into a decidedly crisp night. She would doubtless head for a warm and comforting bed; we, not having befriended the owner of a crash pad, crunched across the beach towards the iodine sea. Breakers drowned the noise of the town. Out there lay Dieppe. Behind us a thousand goddesses were seductively squeezing toothpaste onto brushes. There would be a final combing of the hair, a rinse of the face, then a douche at the bidet before romping through scented darkness towards the naked embrace of a favoured friend. I shuddered to think of it. How distasteful to be excluded from this most basic and necessary of scenarios. I felt like Matthew Arnold declaiming lines from *Dover Beach* :

> Listen! you hear the grating roar
> Of pebbles which the waves draw back, and fling,
> At their return, up the high strand,
> Begin, and cease, and then again begin,
> With tremulous cadence slow, and bring
> The eternal note of sadness in.

I snapped out of my reverie to discover Roger fashioning a depression in the pebbles next to two inverted rowing boats. Then he lay in the hollow and dragged a hull over him. I did likewise some feet away. At least we would be safe from the elements and spared the attention of dossers, druggies, and drunks. During the next six hours we were to sleep fitfully, plagued by phantasmagoria. He was peppered with buckshot and chased by a polar bear. I was a human door a bailiff kept thumping in the back. He was an ice floe from which penguins flopped into the Weddell Sea. I was a pupil whose harsh schoolmarm read aloud from *Cold Comfort Farm*.

We spent the morning of Wednesday 5th July 1967 comatose and bathed by sunlight. Around 2.00 p.m. we got to our feet, intent on missing a second night of perishing discomfort, and rubbed our thoughts together to see what sparks of insight might result. It seemed prudent to head west, which we did for the next few days, subsisting on chocolate and stolen milk and not encountering a bar of soap or a bottle of shampoo. Arriving at Ringwood skint, Roger sought work on a farm and I helped decorate a London couple's holiday bungalow. After ale and a hot pie, I would wander a mile or so south through twilight to the aromatic sanctuary of a bale-packed barn.

By now the lure of blankets and home cooking had become inescapable. We parted amicably, following separate assertions, seeking individual routes back to our mothers. Flush with the proceeds of casual labour, I bought John Betjeman's *Collected Poems* in Salisbury. My parents picked me up slumped outside Chepstow Racecourse, weather-beaten and hirsute. The whimsicality had been enjoyable in a masochistic sense. Irate farmers had chased us for raiding their orchards but we had avoided the attentions of the police. We had also failed to get our end away. The worst episode had been commandeering a rotten boat to ferry us across a filthy creek near Fareham. It had begun to ship water and mudbanks had provided no safe haven. Shaken, we had made it into town. It could have been our quietus.

The Summer of Love was, if not sensational, satisfying: unless you were having the shit kicked out of you in Vietnam. At Greenwich, Queen Elizabeth II knighted round-the-world yachtsman Francis Chichester, and at Clydebank the 58,000-ton liner *Queen Elizabeth II* moved down the slipway. In September, Roger and I and a couple of hundred others returned to Caerleon to begin a new academic year. I was affecting a beard and attempting poetry in earnest, if only with a view to appearing in the college magazine. The periodicals shelf in the library displayed a publication called *London Magazine*. That autumn I sent six poems to its editor, Alan Ross. Within days they came winging back, *Not quite, we felt, but we'd gladly see new ones later* scribbled on the rejection slip. Heartened, I penned more. Some were sent to, daftly, *Reveille*, the *Daily Mail*, and the Beatles Fan Club. The first two were not interested. Freda Kelly, the Fab Four's secretary, replied on 30th November saying *How nice of you to think of us*. She enclosed a machine-autographed photograph of the group, having received some sympathetic drivel occasioned by the death of their manager Brian Epstein. Although my sentiments doubtless ended up in the office bin, this was to be the start of an immense amount of diffuse pestering.

Teaching practices were the one chance we had to put our lecturers' theories to the test. My first, from 19th April to 12th May, had been at St. Julians High School, Newport. Apart from a week at Monmouth Secondary Modern during September, this was to be the sum total of my exposure to sprogs in 1967. For most of March 1968 I was at Portwall Junior School, Chepstow. My third and final practice was at Oakdale Secondary Modern for the autumn term of that year. None of these confrontations proved traumatic, though I could tell that attempting to enlighten teenagers would not be child's play. Around their thirteenth year boys undergo a metamorphosis which would not disgrace a werewolf. Their stature outgrows any choirboy sweetness they might have had, body hair increases, and manners tend to disintegrate. They become harder for parents, teachers, and anyone else invested with authority to handle. It is not a pleasant age.

Oakdale's whippersnappers and bobbysoxers were much nicer than St. Julians' city toughs. Was that because the latter was a single-sex establishment unmellowed by femininity or because Oakdale's homogeneous valley background was more conducive to stable social values? One thing was certain: geometries were more interesting among co-eds. Just as you were tiring of the angularity of dusty-trousered, skewwhiff-tie'd lads, a carefree lass would come round the corner carrying a satchel and a fair ballast of buxomness. Not all puppy fat rendered its owner plain. Properly distributed, it gave the impression of a Rubens model in a uniform two sizes too small. The artist himself had, at the age of fifty-three, married a sixteen-year-old. As a healthy bachelor, I welcomed such attraction wholeheartedly. As a trainee teacher, I frowned thoughtfully.

I had a healthy respect for McNiven and Warne, one-time tutors at Guy's Hospital, who gave to a waiting world *Aids to Obstetric and Gynæcological Nursing*, the nearest I came to erotica during my formative years. Where else could you glimpse those forbidden Islands of the Blessed, the Clitorides, so close to Lesbos yet not on any map of Greece? Nearly everyone found and turned the golden key and entered the sacred darkness sooner or later. All I hoped was that patience would not die before opportunity was born.

That September there was a new intake of talent, most straight from sixth form. I saw in them my former self: nervous, keen to please, uncertain which clubs and societies to join. It was probably their first time away from home. Mummy and Daddy came to settle them into their nice new hostels, whispering on leaving *Be good and if in doubt say no*. Second-year males, however, were prowling wolves, able to ask questions to which 'no' would be the perfect answer. *Would you object to coming out with me this evening?* "Er -

no…." A gleeful rubbing of the hands. *Would you feel shocked if I asked you to visit my room?* "Um - no…." Excellent.

I should have returned on Monday 18th September. Painfully, one quinsied tonsil had a kettle's calcium carbonate about it. Gluteal penicillin jabs were prescribed. I actually returned on Monday 2nd October, refreshed and raring to go. Somehow I was to make little headway but several new acquaintances. Really quite super girls confided in me about their boyfriends. Once or twice I even became a shoulder to cry on. Did that beard make me more avuncular than raunchy? I had marvellous conversations with homely females, most of whom were as virginal as toddlers. All approached sex through the perfumed garden of love and engagement: it would be a final act of surrender. They were theoretically willing to do anything other than let you lay them, for which they could hardly be blamed.

What of the home front? I had until 28th July to Lose It. When that twenty-first birthday arrived only nominal manhood would be attained; the legitimacy of carnal initiation was vital. Would I in desperation be reduced to chatting up unprepossessing shop assistants or to emulating Dustin Hoffman in *The Graduate*, recently released to wide acclaim, by seeking the solace of older women? As if in answer to prayer, something materialised. My father, through his home-based estate agency, managed to interest a young Forest of Dean woman in a particular property and guessed - with chauvinistic brio - she might be fair game for his son.

Joy Wood had left school at fifteen and thought books were for propping up broken dressers. She was not illiterate, only one for whom literacy was unimportant. Her idea of a seminal cultural icon was Cliff Richard. Although not quite on a par with Mary Quant or Zandra Rhodes, she was useful with her hands and could run up a dress in a jiffy. What belied her decent looks was her rural burr, yet she had a kindly disposition and the sort of sunny nature a developed critical faculty might have impaired. We assumed a sort of liaison which juddered through the late spring of 1968. Not wanting me to bum around England pinching fruit again with Roger, my father found me a temporary job. I was to assist in the Warren Wing of the Dilke Memorial Hospital, Cinderford for several weeks and would receive accommodation, food, and a moderate wage. When I discovered it to be a twilight ward for old fogies I was less than thrilled. This was the Era of Youth. It was the threshold of liberation for Czechoslovakia, France, the world. Tariq Ali and Daniel Cohn-Bendit were storming Establishment barricades, Mick Jagger was belting out *Jumping Jack Flash*, and I was attending to geriatrics. Had my father been untouched by flower power? Was he impervious to Tiny Tim tiptoeing through the tulips or to Arthur Brown on fire, Janis Joplin's acid rock or the ending of British stage censorship? He had clearly forgotten 1927 and how it felt to be two decades young. Had he not marvelled at Charles Lindbergh's solo Atlantic flight or the *Flying Scotsman* thundering non-stop from King's Cross to Newcastle? Had he not whooped at the opening of the first automatic telephone exchange or wept at the death of ex-King Ferdinand of Rumania? I jibbed, mildly. Anything stronger and I would have been bawled out. While contemporaries were grooving to Cream's latest album *Disraeli Gears* I was returning to bedpans and dentures. The long vac was upon us and that fateful birthday was nearing.

I thought she was a virgo intacta though could not be sure. I was troubled by several things. What, for example, had happened to her father? She refused to say. She lived at home with her mother and two brothers but where was dad? Behind the hospital in a spartan room overlooking dense woodland we lay, only necking - so far. She was quiescent, yielding easily yet merely wetting her toes: paddling in passion not diving through it. Then a note came via an intermediary. Matron was cross because I was 'consorting' on the premises. Girlfriends were *verboten*. We must meet elsewhere. So much for spinsterish edicts. Again I had no option other than to obey.

As much through anger and frustration as through lust, I invited her home for the weekend. She arrived on Friday 12th July and slept in the front room. Next day I told my parents we were hitching to Bath. Before they could protest we had gone, walking two miles to Trellech and the B4293. We got a lift to the Severn Bridge and another to our destination. So it was that on the evening of the 13th I hesitantly approached the portals of the Royal York Hotel on George Street, a packet of Durex in my pocket, my heart stomping like a giant. I sidled up to the receptionist.

"Can I help you, sir?"

"We'd like a room for the night. Double, that is."

Elegant fingers riffled through the ledger. "I'm afraid all doubles are taken but I can offer you a twin-bedded."

"Y-yes, that'll do nicely."

She smiled. "What name please?"

"Name? Oh - my name.... It's Blewitt. A Mr. Blewitt. And this is my wife, Mrs. Blewitt. We *are* married, you know."

"I don't doubt it, sir. Here's your key. Room 30. Henry will take your bags. Breakfast is at..."

"We don't have any luggage," I blurted, and made for the stairs. A smirking porter barred our ascent with brusque efficiency.

"Do you know where you're going, sir?" I stalled, unsure whether to say yes or no. "Allow me." He led the way with, I thought, exaggerated slowness. Room 27, Room 28, Room 29.... I held my breath. This was it.

He inserted the key and opened the door. A whiff of stale air egressed. No urns of fruit or Nubian slaves with palms, pet cheetahs, and sumptuous garments met our gaze, only what you would expect in this type of traditional establishment. £5. 2s. 3d's worth of fulfilment! He stood ramrod straight, adjusting his tie and meaningfully clearing his throat. I slipped him half-a-crown for carrying nothing, and he nodded, backing out gracefully.

The first thing I did was slide the sash up. It gave onto

noisy Broad Street. My left hand held her right, my right her left: a pleasing symmetry. Our lips met briefly. "I'll sleep here," I announced, claiming the bed nearer the window. She looked in the wardrobe, being clothes conscious. Perhaps she hoped to find a forgotten Yves Saint Laurent classic draped over a metal hangar.

Using the soap and towels provided, I washed the sheen from my face, and combed my hair. She did likewise while I lay on the bed, ankles crossed, hands behind head. We could have Done It in a field somewhere but I would have had to have made the running and she might have said no. She still had not said yes. I figured it was essentially a matter of logistics. Pluck her from familiar surroundings and she would feel more solidarity with me. Get some decent food and drink down her. Use mellow tiredness to erode her resolve. Then produce the magic prophylactics to prove there would be no lasting effects. Under the guise of darkness, and having shed our clothes for bed, it should be less hassle than visiting the dentist. In theory. That was all the uninitiated had to go on.

It was already the middle of the evening and neither of us knew where the nearest inexpensive restaurant was. Eventually we found somewhere genial and unostentatious and ate lustily. I recalled Albert Finney and Joyce Redman gorging themselves lasciviously in *Tom Jones*, Tony Richardson's rambunctious film of five years before. When we re-entered the foyer at 10.40 all was quiet. A different receptionist was in place, painting her nails. We crept upstairs and along the hushed corridor. I breathlessly unlocked the door, feeling brave and reckless. She uncertainly followed.

I hung my jacket on a chair, then took off my tie and shirt. Stripped to the waist, I discarded my shoes, pairing them neatly. I unbelted my trousers and let them drop. Next I hurriedly cleaned my teeth. Finally I climbed into bed and removed my Y-fronts and socks under the sheet. Naked at last - and in the same room as a woman! She killed the light and took off various elastic and nylon garments some distance away. I shivered. Goose flesh on a warm night! So it was to happen in Bath, close to the scene of a less fruitful entanglement with Jane Sheppard eighteen months before. Suddenly she was a silvery statue, an ivory Galatea among the shadows. She slipped between her sheets. There was nothing to say. I carefully lifted my jacket and took the packet from the pocket. Everything became studiedly tactile. Fumbling fingers tore at the sachet. Out flopped the greasy rubber loop.

I crossed the three-foot gap between us, lifted her sheet, and slid beneath. She also had a single blanket; another lay folded nearby. Geographical exploration ensued. I had read the textbooks and perused the maps. Here was the head, face uppermost; isthmus neck; cliff shoulders; hill breasts; desert belly with oasis navel. My right hand continued, an intrepid traveller. Her pelvis presented a mountain ridge. Then came scrub, prelude to the tropical rift valley and its fertile secrets. The further south I penetrated the more ardent became our embrace. When finally my hand touched the holy of holies she matured into a wonderful vehemence. By now I felt as if I had the Horn of Africa. On rolled the lubricious contraption. Next I positioned myself like a missionary, weight on elbows. I eased her knees up. A penile lunge achieved nothing. The range finder was adjusted by a few degrees. A second lunge. No luck. Generously she helped me, and I was in. It felt the same as being out, only tighter; at least you could not veer to right or left, only go backward and forward - like trying to push a loaded wheelbarrow up a plank. Backward and forward, backward and forwards.... Establish a rhythm. Backwards and forwards. They had been doing this hereabouts since a settlement named after the Celtic goddess Sul was founded AD 48. The water for its residents originated as springs in the Mendip Hills, whose underground streams collected mineral salts as they flowed. All I could think of were hidden sumps and passageways. That, coupled with the effects of the Frascati we had had with our meal, lulled me until the metaphors became maritime, her regular gasps a galleon's creaking timbers. Just then a great wave inundated us and we sank together through the depths of consciousness.

I do not know how long we lay without moving. She had straightened her legs. I remained *in situ* like a gluttonous bullfrog stupefied by marsh gas. We were glued by mutual sweat; our sexuality smelt like Chanel No. 5 poured over tuna. Her heart was someone running up a fire escape. The firm line of her jaw pressed my right ear. She clasped my shoulders. There was nothing now to hide. We had come clean with each other. Keats had contracted gonorrhoea, Schubert syphilis. We would be untainted by the experience.

I shifted my weight, and rolled alongside. She nestled in my arms and I hauled the sheet and blanket properly over us. Before we could fall asleep romantically entwined I had to deal with the condom. I went to the sink and pulled the shaving-light cord. They say ejaculating elephants produce a litre of spermatic fluid. The pathetic exhibit that lay in my palm contained barely enough to cosh a gnat. I tied a knot in the thing and dropped it in the bin, contenting myself with the hypothesis that chambermaids get used to such finds. Animality had finally triumphed. Californian sea otters bite their partner's nose during copulation; captive male tigers must be screened from their mates afterwards to avoid being mauled. By contrast the indistinct shape in the bed behind me was as harmless as lard.

Next day Mr. and Mrs. Blewitt sat calmly at breakfast. A fat American couple nearby did not notice us, nor did a party of subdued businessmen, several of whom looked hung over. We kept glancing to left and right, half expecting relatives to appear shaking their fists like characters from an H.M. Bateman cartoon, as if we had been the guests who had called 'pâté de foie gras' potted meat.

I indulged my new-found hard-won freedom to the full, utilising any and every opportunity with relish, embarrassing scores of shop assistants with demands for what still lay, in many chemists, discreetly out of view. She was perfectly happy to be a minor Henry Miller character speaking the local vernacular. The summer had not been wasted despite its unpromising start. I strutted into my final academic year like the cat that swallowed the cream, convincing myself females would now fling themselves before me, somehow intuiting my state of enhanced manhood from my exaggerated gait.

8

This is to be the image: square-jawed, laid-back, jingling a handful of change in one's trousers rather than worriedly playing pocket pool. I swing from lianas of the mind, emitting a resonant war cry - "Hi, gorgeous." But she looks through me, unimpressed. September's intake have arrived. It is the Caerleon equivalent of a Freshers' Ball. Spirits run high.

I shift my gaze elsewhere. "What's your name?"

"Gly - nis," comes the reply, a cupful of the River Tawe poured slowly over my head. I clear my throat and move on. There, two-thirds shadow, one-third purple light, stands a paragon of pulchritude. I sidle up to her.

"You're new, aren't you?" She laughs, showing perfect violet teeth, and answers in Received Pronunciation. "Um, this is the start of my third year," I continue. She cranes forward in profile, squinting. Blast the music! How can one converse against this din? I approach the immaculate shell of her ear with the urgency of Pheidippides, resenting the irony - for the disc is the Bee Gees' current smash *I've Gotta Get A Message To You*. I take her gently by the arm towards the rear of the hall. She looks away anxiously for a moment, then relaxes as her bloke arrives with two Cokes. I shrug and smile resignedly.

She does the same. He scowls. This is futile. Only if one is adept at sign language and has first-rate night vision does one stand a chance here. The anteroom is brighter, marginally quieter, and clogged with bodies, through which I step, a ballerina between cowpats. There is a queue at the coffee machine, which I am relieved to see is not out of order. I nod amiably at known associates but my eyes are for the jenny-come-latelies, most of whom are overgrown girls rather than attractive women. A male acquaintance introduces me to an exception: Priscilla Holdaway.

"Allow me to buy you a drink," I say with the solicitude of a favourite uncle. She agrees and we get talking. I flip when told where she is from. What is she doing *here*? Corner this cookie and it'll be constitutionals down that famous drive to the statuary at its foot, champagne on the lawn, and glimpses of Nancy Astor engaging Neville Chamberlain in spectral debate. "I'm sorry, I thought you said *Cliveden*. Clevedon's quite another matter." I cast about inside my head.

"It's on the other side of the Bristol Channel," she says to ease my perplexity.

"Ah...." I sound like a punctured rugby ball.

"Anyway," says the third party, "I'll leave you to it." Our go-between departs and we wander from the overdone ending of *Hey Jude*, the Beatles' fifteenth chart-topper. Immediately I recognise something too often lacking in my own performance: intelligence. In this instance it's married to good looks and full-blooded self-assurance. Soon I learn of Clevedon Court where Thackeray wrote much of *Vanity Fair* and where John Betjeman visited his friend Arthur Elton, whose ancestral home it was. I say I should like to see the town sometime. She enthuses about the walks she takes with her dog Danny. I strain at the leash. We stroll to her hostel, parting on an upbeat note. We've clicked!

We firm up our affinity next day when I meet her ambling along a corridor bearing an armful of books. Her face glows with recognition.

"Let me carry those." She smiles and sighs with relief. "Off to a lecture?" She nods. I turn on my heel and escort her to the classroom. We arrange to meet at eight for drinks in The Red Lion.

At eleven that night, sated with lassitude and lager, we kiss somewhat chastely. Soon it will be the weekend and a chance to enter that concrete-and-glass Xanadu where the female students live. This I do without any arm-twisting. Her room is neat and comfortable. She boils a kettle, produces two mugs, and opens a packet of garibaldis. What do I notice? Built-in wardrobe, easy chair, holiday postcards, wastepaper basket, writing unit…. I recline on the bed as if signalling intent. Here she spends a third of her time; this is the pillow her head indents for eight-hour stretches. What do I make of her? She is as well-proportioned as the Venus de Milo *and* has arms. Her teeth are strong, her eyes are bright, she has a slight Somerset accent, her personality is breezy and positive. She has passed A-level English at A grade and did creditably in a couple of other subjects. Her father works for Rolls-Royce Aero Engines in Bristol and she has a brother named Jon. Other family members include her mother and a cat called Teddy.

For several months we are inseparable. We accompany each other to dances, eat together in the dining hall, relax together in television lounges, shop together in Newport, sit together in the grounds, and discuss lectures, essays, teaching practices, fellow students, and the folks back home. Soon I get to see Clevedon's graceful Victorian wrought-iron pier, its Georgian and Regency buildings, its quaint shops. She lives along Kings Road. Her parents are pleasant; her brother is unpesky. I even like her dog. I begin to think a long-term relationship may have arrived. Where's the fly in the ointment? What of the godfather, that well-meaning but overbearing gentleman back at The Narth who must vet all liaisons before I proceed with them?

When she visits, her routine is to bus to Chepstow where we pick her up in the estate car. Much as dad appears to like her, it's clear he prefers the Forest of Dean miss I whisked off to Bath. This new arrival has too much nous. Moreover, her father's salary dwarfs my father's pension; meeting on equal terms will prove impossible, despite my parents' business being increasingly lucrative. I recognise this but can do nothing about it.

Such concerns are peripheral to our uncomplicated canoodling in her hostel room behind drawn blinds. She is a battleground where primness meets passion. One Saturday afternoon, with a great effort of will, she strips to her knickers. Her body is good enough to eat. Her breasts are full and round without being heavy. My God, she's beautiful - and steamy. I am prepared to overlook her habit of quoting John Donne during moments of intimacy. By any estimate we are well up the ladder to the stars. The next steps are crucial. Complete exposure is the sticking point, with good reason. Her head, if not her heart, is setting limits. I wheedle and cajole, swearing no harm will ensue if she submits, and saying this remains the last obstacle to total immersion in each other's psyche. More effort must be expended before those Marks and Sparks briefs are shed. Finally the moment arrives. Simultaneously numerous Caerleon hearties are attempting to score a try, engaging in foul play, aiming for goal, mauling, worrying about obstruction, and finding themselves offside - our predicament exactly.

Around us volcanic pools of desire bubble. Our heated fondling never reaches the *ne plus ultra*. We could do it, we should do it, but we don't. Our exertions are safe, sensual, and only partially satisfying. In the shadows, John Donne declaims:

> *License my roving hands, and let them go,*
> *before, behind, between, above, below.*

She does and that's it. All is not lost. Time, to echo the Rolling Stones, is on our side, even though this year I leave college while she stays. We vow to trade letters regularly and to visit each other's home on alternate weekends. She finds holiday work at the Hales cake factory in Clevedon. I seek job interviews and look for a second-hand car. Question marks proliferate. Out of sight, out of mind. Absence makes the heart grow fonder. Which is truer? In a more chivalrous age the latter was. Nowadays what is readily available trumps what is not. The first maxim is six centuries the older and explains the crusaders' need for chastity belts. Early attempts at computerised translation rendered it *Blind and mad*. I ask for a personal means of transport to Clevedon but my father doesn't fork out £85·00 for a 1962 Ford Anglia van until the following spring, by which time our young hearts have not grown fonder. With neat dovetailing, no temporal shortfall, and a rattan bridge across the Himalayan torrent of our immaturity we could make it. We have potential yet slip through each other's grasp because of distance and parental disinclination. This shows later in the summer.

She reads J.D. Salinger's novel *The Catcher in the Rye* and dislikes its abrupt ending. She looks forward to the televised Investiture of the Prince of Wales at Caernarvon Castle despite, or because of, the Free Wales Army's threat of violence. Her next book is Jean-Paul Sartre's *The Age of Reason*. Our letters cross. I say I have just hitched back from staying with Roger Griffiths and his wife Jackie. They married while at Caerleon and left to seek their fortune in London. I tick to her and she tocks to me, a pendulum across the Severn Estuary. My father frowns. He can put his arm around the local lass and joke with her, but this young woman's a different proposition. Does he really want her for a daughter-in-law? No. I must stop seeing her. "Why?" I bleat lamely. His face turns to stone and his brows are heavy. He says we are getting too involved. She wants me to phone frequently. He resents this: calls cost money. Besides, he is always dialling clients or putting bets through to his bookmaker. He is more interested in *Persian War*, the racehorse that rewards him handsomely by winning the Champion Hurdle in both 1968 and 1969. She sends another missive, enclosing a magazine cutting: 'F.L. of Camberley writes *My handwriting is pretty scrawly. Is it good manners to type a love letter?* An agony aunt replies: *It isn't regarded as good manners to type ANY personal letter - or acceptances of invitations.*' Point taken. She sends snaps of her on the lawn cuddling Danny. Charles Philip Arthur George and his mother do not get targeted by terrorists. I buy a chant recorded in Room 1742 of Hotel La Reine Elizabeth, Montreal. Its message: give peace a chance. When next I return from Priscilla's my father refuses to meet me in Chepstow. I overnight at The George Hotel; it sets me back 42 shillings and 17 pence. For my birthday she gives me W. Somerset Maugham's *Of Human Bondage*. Irrespective of the date of hers, I reciprocate with a book on English cathedrals. It is the mind-blowing summer of Woodstock and the Isle of Wight festival. I attend Bob Dylan's appearance at the latter. Three days after the death of group member Brian Jones the Rolling Stones perform free in Hyde Park. Although she invites me to stay for the weekend I trek up to the massive open-air concert. This provokes her ire. Her father phones to tell me so. My father retorts "What a confounded cheek!" and dictates a stiff letter to the Holdaways ending our liaison. He tells me to sign it. I reluctantly comply.

9

Within this maelstrom a still small voice urges 'Do not start teaching, despite that glorious T. Cert. after your name. Continue formal education, eventually leading not children to maturity but adults to salvation'. To my surprise, my application to train for ordination is accepted. I commence studies on Monday 6th October 1969 at St. Michael & All Angels Theological College, Llandaff. Since 1958 my life has swung from the sublime to the ridiculous and back again: six years in a mixed environment to seven in an all-male environment to one in an all-female environment to three in a mixed environment to the likelihood of two in an all-male environment. Having postponed the evil day of having to earn a living, I am delivered to the seminary by my parents on the afternoon of Sunday 5th October. What I remember are august entrances and dust devils, dying leaves and traffic fumes. Beyond the portals one is becalmed in a contemplative enclave.

We trek to the modernistic chapel thrice daily; meditation and silent reading are also undertaken within its austere walls. Caerleon had no such edifice. If it had it would have resounded to bowdlerised rugby songs sung, hand on heart, in the best valleys' tradition, though I admit to finding the image of cassocked prop forwards mildly distasteful. St. Michael & All Angels (it never really feels like St Mike's) resembles an Oxbridge college rooted in Welsh soil. The current of fun here might not make the voltmeter flicker if the prospectus is to be believed. Students 'will remember that many things expedient and lawful elsewhere must be surrendered in a theological college, and should not expect to enjoy a regular round of pleasures and social entertainments'. It's going to be more the can't-can't than the can-can. 'During lectures or study hours quiet must be observed in the College.' What about my stack of pop LPs? 'Students are asked to practise economy in the matter of light and fuel.' Is that it? There's a chilling rider: 'The College reserves the right to ask any student to leave, not only on moral or disciplinary grounds but also if it is felt to be in the best interests of the College.'

Do I remain poker-faced or throw in my hand now? Let us not prejudge. We have six terms in which to adapt to the peculiar rigours of the place. The fact that elsewhere the sixties continue to swing is immaterial. Many things are immaterial here. Having thought Compline a digestible food for invalids, I find it a severely simple service unaccompanied by organ. Plainsong flourishes about us like cabbage whites above an allotment. We stand grimly and repeat the sentences with heavy monastic hearts. This is widely at variance with the Kingsley Amis novel I'm reading (*I Want It Now*) and the type of film I've watched over the last six months: Jean-Luc Godard's *Masculin-Féminin*, Mike Nichols' *The Graduate*, Milos Forman's *The Fireman's Ball*.... I regale a fellow student with the old joke about why firemen have bigger balls than policemen. He responds with such shock that I shrink from his gaze and leave the room.

The day starts early - too early. I stagger out of my bedroom, rub the sleep from my eyes, and perform ablutions with numerous others. The small talk of fledgling vicars at dawn, though mind-numbingly banal, is at least clean. Sanitised, in fact. After Morning Prayer we break our fast on the usual fare: tea, cornflakes, bacon and egg, toast and marmalade. At high table sits Warden Rees, known to all and sundry as Og after his initials and the Old Testament king of Bashan. The highlight of the academic year is when a passage containing the name is read from the lectern in his presence. Pew-fellows chuckle heartily, and Og looks smug, bashful, or bored depending on his mood. Owen Geoffrey Rees gives regular tutorials in his book-lined study. I find him likeable and straightforward beneath the scholarly carapace. Unnervingly, he appears to have read most of the thousand or so arcane volumes ranged around the walls. Often he will spring from his Windsor chair, pluck a title from a shelf, and seek a corroborative text. This puts you off making unguarded comments. His words unerringly hit their target; yours weave giddily towards uncertain conclusions. Doubt is unknown to him. He's weighed every theological issue and arrived at a sound opinion on them all. His colleagues are no slouches either. John Mears, sub-warden and later Bishop of

Bangor, discharges his responsibilities creditably. Colin Sykes, the librarian, is an affable egghead. Michael Bowles teaches New Testament Greek with energetic briskness. He really grabs you by the synoptics. We are asked to regard philosophy and Christianity with equal seriousness though one leads to growing doubt, the other to glowing certainty. They are beasts straining in opposite directions. The result is uneasy stasis. Apply the dispassionate thinker's methodology too rigorously and you will be accused of faithlessness. No one seems able or willing to resolve this crux. That apart, little rocks our sturdy Galilean boat. The waters of the lake stay eerily placid.

What of the other ordinands? Where do they get their kicks? The answer has a leaden literalness. Soccer. Nobody knows I have not booted a ball in years. They ask what position I play. With a blasé shrug I say, "Striker." Our first game is on Wednesday 22nd October at 2.30 on Pontcanna Fields, a large area of suburban greenness beside the River Taff. The hour arrives. Sunshine burnishes the trees and warms the leaf-mould-scented air. Just down the road, angels more real than anything in the Good Book file in orderly fashion to their lessons at Howell's, a member of the Girls' Public Day School Trust. For over a century the establishment has produced well-turned-out young ladies on its genteel conveyor belt. I borrow some kit and worry briefly about contracting crab lice. This irrational fear is overshadowed by the fact that footballers occasionally get hurt. There's a real chance I could, as inside right, become ambulance fodder. Might I seek exemption by avowedly having to finish an extended essay? This rather necessitates starting one, none having been set. Should I allot myself something like *Examine the Role of Tractarianism in Twentieth-Century Thought* or *The Pseudepigrapha: A Critical Assessment*? Fellow divines are on their way to the field. I swallow hard and join them.

How better for these clean-cut youths to balance their sanctity than by muddying their knees! A whistle signifies the start of the first half. Rays filter reassuringly through russet branches yet already I'm perspiring - despite Ezekiel 44:18 advising, in relation to players, 'They shall not gird themselves with any thing that causeth sweat'. A few supporters spur us on by deriding our opponents, who bring to mind Jeremiah 5:6: 'Their transgressions are many and their backslidings are great'. However, Isaiah 22:18 provides a serious threat as regards my opposite number: 'He will surely violently turn and toss thee like a ball.... There shalt thou die'. A winger shouts my name and the confounded leather orb whizzes towards me. I close my eyes, grit my teeth, and kick. "You clot!" someone yells. I open them. Twenty-one heated players grimace. The ball floats serenely downriver. The next ten minutes are spent trying to retrieve it. Eventually the elusive ellipsoid is brought ashore. After an unholy bollocking I am sent towards the touchline where my substitute eagerly runs on the spot.

Ostensibly, St. Michael & All Angels is intellectually liberal. Engage in debate and you will discover dyed-in-the-wool conservatism. Anyone who wants to spend half the night discussing Nietzsche is going to be disappointed. Formalism is all. You need not study controversial thinkers or theologians; just repeat the routine without whinging and you'll end up in a nice little curacy comforting old ladies, visiting the sick ("Mmn, those grapes look nice. May I?"), and helping choirboys part their hair ("You must keep *still*, Dominic"). Originality is discouraged. Psychical research does not get a look-in. Other religions are ignored. Although the likes of A.J. Ayer, Karl Barth, Reinhold Niebuhr, Gilbert Ryle, Pierre Teilhard de Chardin, and Ludwig Wittgenstein are noted across a crowded room they are not buttonholed. Should they be? Arguably, yes. Instead we get talked at in a breezy, slightly condescending way, as if our century has licked most metaphysical problems. I hear the superior chuckle of John Robinson, 'fearless' Bishop of Woolwich, reverberating around the building. Writing about divine retribution, he states, 'In a real sense the definition of heaven and hell is the same: being with God - for ever. For some that's heaven, for some it's hell: for most of us it's a bit of both.' He dispenses with Hieronymus Bosch's unsettling *oeuvre*, demons get flushed down the pan, and the Almighty becomes the ultimate colleague of good and bad alike. It's wonderful being with Him if you're virtuous. He's a darned nuisance if you're not. History's monsters get stuck in Paradise and must suffer its blessings for eternity.

In order to combat monotony and rejoin the real world, Aled Williams and I escape whenever possible. His fiancée Eirian boards nearby and teaches in Senghenydd. He hails from Aberystwyth, has an Agricultural Science degree, is likeable, down-to-earth, and bilingual, and can smell a rat a mile off. After Saturday Compline he and I do not retire to our rooms to contemplate our navel but creep through a side gate, slide into his van, and visit a strip club near Bute Street. It's an execrable place (smoky, loud, harshly lit, and peopled by rogues and whores) yet a blessed relief after the strait-laced constraint of college.

A scratchy record - Louis Armstrong, Shirley Bassey, Johnny Mathis - starts, and a woman shambles onto the low stage a few feet from us. Her complexion is pasty, her hair is bleached, and her eyebrows have been plucked to extinction. She wears a tight black miniskirt with a scarlet blouse, and gyrates with studied indifference, eventually kicking off a shoe. Another joins it. She sighs with relief or boredom, fumbles at her neck, and undoes a hook and eye. Soon she crosses her arms and lifts the upper garment to reveal a pale stomach and lacy bra. A few dockers, pimps, and spivs shout encouragement. She grins, showing imperfect dentition. Her PVC skirt is unzipped, and falls to the floor. Her legs are on the thin side, and she has an appendicectomy scar. The stylus sticks. We grind to a halt. Someone gives the B side an airing. Fishnet stockings are rolled down, and the crimson brassiere is shed with hammy coyness. Her breasts are small. She doffs the matching pants and suspender belt, opens her legs, and gives a stiff pelvic thrust. There is scant pubic hair. I glimpse the wrinkled furrow of her vulva, and down the remains of my warm beer. She disappears behind a faded curtain to perfunctory applause. It is approaching midnight.

Whether Aled goes further than 'Rwy'n dy garu di' with his betrothed I cannot tell. *I love you* sounds great in any language yet I seem not to have heard it for ages. Two years in Llandaff will hardly fill my little black book with intriguing telephone numbers. The only Numbers here contains thirty-six chapters and the chilling text 'Be sure your sin will find you out'. Somehow we don't feel guilty about our visits to the clip joint. It's an antidote to the po-facedness of our immediate surroundings. Virtually all our peers are virgins. Many would rather bed Foxe's *Book of Martyrs* than a Sandie Shaw lookalike. At the weekend, girlfriends drop by for tea and cake. Most are dumpy, bespectacled, and unimaginative.

After twenty-two years of existence I'm untainted by avarice, rarely envious, hardly gluttonous, seldom proud of myself, and neither slothful nor wrathful, yet I do admit to the debilitating presence of lust. The current nine days' filmic wonder is not Pier Paolo Pasolini's austere *The Gospel According to Saint Matthew* but Vilgot Sjoman's flashy *I Am Curious Yellow*. The gutter press is agog. *The Western Mail* says it's showing at 7.00 in a fleapit two miles away. After dinner at 6.00 I hurry through a warren of streets in order to catch this steamy Scandinavian sexport, and arrive soaked in sweat. Someone has boobed. The 1961 comedy *Come September* with Rock Hudson and Gina Lollobrigida is showing instead. I stump in, slap down the money on the counter, and buy a ticket. Just behind me for its duration a young couple breathlessly grope. I fume at the irony of the situation.

Morning, noon, and night the doxologies continue. Although we all like praise, from the humblest punkah-wallah to the hardiest sheepdog, surely God does not require constantly to be told how wonderful He is. What counts is whether we are heliotropic or selenotropic, growing healthily towards light or reaching up unnaturally through darkness. Asceticism is the equivalent of putting a pot plant on the bare boards of an empty room. Its home is in the garden with its kith and kin. Am I wrong? Certainly I am ignorant. Most here are familiar with the unfamiliar. My first meeting with the word 'pyx' is in Philip Larkin's poem 'Church Going', and I have never come across the word 'paten'. What is an antependium, or the difference between a tau cross and a saltire cross? Am I cut out for this sort of thing? Soon we'll be needing leather kneepads. I knock on Aled's door as the sun is high and we have an afternoon off. He's elsewhere, probably with his intended. In the quad a snail moves over the pavement. Rooks laugh from high elms or swirl in vortices of freedom. The library beckons. Should I spend my spare time probing Rudolf Bultmann's existential theology? Will it catapult me to glory or induce myopia? I resignedly climb the wide wooden staircase to find out.

We are robing in the sacristy then proceeding to the nave, led by a lily-white crucifer, acolytes and choristers blending voices agreeably. A great concrete whalebone arches over the aisle, supporting an aluminium *Christ in Majesty*. Jacob Epstein, its executor, had been way ahead of his time. Not surprisingly, he was excluded from the Royal Society of British Sculptors and the Royal Academy. Here in Llandaff Cathedral his handiwork soars. We enter the choir stalls, the strains of 'Jesus calls us: o'er the tumult' subsiding in echoes of echoes. This, apart from applying poultices to the sores of Bombay beggars, is what Christianity is all about: having an aesthetic high, attuning oneself to the power of decent music in a respectable setting where the crazed tinkle of ice-cream vans and the land mines of dog turds are forever absent. Moreover, you cannot see one council house, one *News of the World*, or one set of heated rollers. It's a middle-class wet dream.

If I get through this course alive I might plump for the

lifestyle of the poet R. S. Thomas (who was once a student here) by pacing the primeval mountains of mid-Wales clad in a swirling cloak of mist, steely eyes piercing the gloom as if to perceive Rhiannon's birds whose singing held listeners spellbound, or Branwen who died of grief after her brother's beheading. Part of me warms to the escapist attraction of being a Cambrian shepherd tending his human flock, trudging - lantern in hand - to some outlandish hill farm where time stands still and a gnarled presence sets phlegm sizzling in the grate. Ten to one the reality would be a tedious little number near Bridgend, succouring single mums and snotty-nosed kids on a sump estate. Thoughts drift back to the present as the congregation stands with the sound of stampeding bison to sing its next roof-raiser.

I resolve to establish a stable liaison as soon as possible to avoid resorting to self-abuse, a practice condemned alike by the Egyptians around 1,500 BC in their collection of religious and magical texts *The Book of the Dead* and by Bekker in 1741 ('Masturbation... an abominable custom, a horrible sin, results in black-yellowish and leaden complexion, paroxysm, desiccation, emaciation, sterility, frigidity'). To this end I re-establish contact with Maureen Moss who I had met at Caerleon College. We trade letters, especially since she lives in Caerphilly, close enough for us to follow them up. If my room - No. 24 - could double as a lothario's den there might be a satisfactory denouement. The task is difficult for she wears vestal chain mail and these surroundings are hardly designed for seduction.

I suppose we could click if marooned on a desert island. As things stand she is precious and careful and I'm importunate and heedless of the niceties of conventional courtship. It would be unfair to deride her for idolising American vocalist Andy Williams or for having crushes on actors Peter O'Toole, Edward Woodward, and Paul Newman, yet just as she cannot rest her affection on any celebrity in particular so she cannot settle for a single boyfriend. Her drearily simplistic strategy is to fuel the ardour of several by playing one off against the other. This may work with dishy models like Jean Shrimpton or Twiggy but it is overly optimistic to expect the ploy to be equally efficacious with the unastonishing offspring of a lollipop lady and a British Rail workman. Like many girls I've met she has great potential, but it would take two years with Voluntary Service Overseas to iron out the wrinkles of smug affectation. What's likelier is she'll get engaged to one of her doting suitors and lose her cherry on her wedding night. She is currently stringing along Geraint and Graham and Malcolm and, to some extent, me.

Someone taps my shoulder after ninety minutes of juggling to no avail with the cosmological, moral, ontological, and teleological arguments for the existence of God. Bleary-eyed, I turn. He wants 1s 6d off me as they're having a Miss World sweepstake. I cough up and find I have been lumbered with Miss Dominican Republic, who will doubtless be so Hispanic as to make a dog's dinner out of answering the Master of Ceremonies' questions. It's nice to know my colleagues aren't entirely wrapped up in Second Timothy. I count my cash. There could be enough for another trip to the Ringside Club. It's ten bob at the door so I'd better be tightfisted for a day or two. When the ordinands circulate the Biafran Famine collection tin I'll drop in a load of ha'pennies on the sly; they ceased being legal tender on 31st July. Wait - no strip joint merits stooping so low. Maureen says she's just been to her local nightspot, the Checkmate Club, with some ardent admirer. I tell her *Les Cousins* in Greek Street would be infinitely superior, with membership at half-a-crown and admission from five shillings depending on which performers are appearing. She is unimpressed. I change tack. "Are Jane Birkin and Serge Gainsbourg really at it on the hit single *Je T'Aime… Moi Non Plus* ?" She looks at me with blithe incomprehension. A smoker would fumble dispiritedly for a cigarette. I reach, almost reflexively, for a gospel commentary.

I continue fiddling around with verse, also a capricious

dame. B.S. Johnson, editor and experimental novelist, takes 'Squares' for *Transatlantic Review*. My three-guinea payment feels like a pools win. Then Derek Parker accepts 'Victim' for *Poetry Review* so the decade finishes on a high, provided this year's twenty-three rejections are conveniently overlooked. At this rate, I kid myself, publication in book form will come by the time I'm twenty-seven, Seamus Heaney's age when his first Faber & Faber volume appeared. It'll certainly happen by the time I'm thirty. A Tennysonian career seems assured. Why are those rooks still laughing in the tall trees, feathered Lord Haw-Haws?

Miss Moss ends her first letter with 'Very best wishes', her twelfth with 'Love'. I still haven't so much as given her a blast of halitosis. It's all in the mind, which sounds like a kiss's definition: application at headquarters for a job at base. I recommend London. Surely she'd like us to go there fairly soon. My idea, obviously, is to book into a small hotel once we realise we've missed the last train home. If I can ply her with a meal and enough of her favourite port-and-lemons it might just be possible to get my rocks off. She says, having checked with her parents, "It seems we'll only to be able to manage a day trip. Do you think we can see all the sights?" Oh yeah, no problem.

My ambition to consign the sixties to history more with a bang than a whimper founders. Apart from a cheap Christmas card the only word from her is a censorious screed on 5th January. Time's passing veils St. Michael's yuletide party, after which it seems I inveigle her to my room and pounce, the crucifix on the wall and the noble tomes along the shelves adding a surreal piquancy to the goings-on. I'm sure it's no more than suggestive playfulness, but henceforth she would prefer 'a relationship of the mind' (one of the crummiest conceits ever). And if it's one-track, what then? Bobbie Gentry's chart-topper *I'll Never Fall In Love Again* presents a note of personal foreboding. It is with mixed feelings that I let Geraint and Graham and Malcolm (and, yes, Alan and Gary and some nameless Eyetie) get on with it, and may the best flank forward win.

Bored with most facets of my current position, I resolve to leave the neat little seminarians to their own devices, Lady Bountiful to hers, and Cardiff to its. Philosophers David Hume and Immanuel Kant were right. Reason, they said, cannot demonstrate God's existence, though a belief in Him supports hope, morality, and society. It is time to write to Archdeacon Ivor of Newport and Bishop Stephen of Monmouth. The reason I'm curtailing my commitment is ostensibly because my father has developed a heart condition and I must help mother run the family business. Both letters are received sympathetically. I pack cassock, surplice, and Bible, click shut the suitcase, and walk from the college to join the busy world outside. A hundred yards away a public house beckons. Yes, there's just time for a quick one at the Maltsters Arms.

10

Work's main redeeming feature is you get paid for it. Mostly it's a matter of selling yourself for money. Because of various Judaeo-Christian pronouncements this is considered less tacky than mainline whoring. During the Middle Ages poverty was regarded as blessed, an idea supported by the Sermon on the Mount. Later it was put about that financial success was more pleasing to Heaven. German sociologist Max Weber went so far as to ascribe the rise of capitalism to Calvinism, a creed which declares the daily grind little short of godly.

My first teaching post is at Lydney, Gloucestershire. I am quite keen to sprinkle a younger generation from the watering can of knowledge. Will such labour repay idealism or gradually erode it until I become just another hack peda-gogue? Time, to quote the truism, will tell. When it does I hope there'll be enough left in which to act accordingly.

As it's impossible to reach my destination by public transport from The Narth, toil for seven hours, then return in like manner, my father buys me a van. The mileometer has a daunting row of numbers yet the engine sounds as sweet as the music of the spheres. My route winds down through pretty Whitebrook, crosses the Wye at Bigsweir, and ascends through the hamlets of Mork and Stowe. Evenings are given over to television and marking books. After Caerleon and Cardiff, socialising stagnates. Most school friends are married and many have dispersed. For leisure I retreat into the composition of chess problems and doggerel. C.H.O'D. Alexander, International Master, twice British Champion, and *Sunday Times* games guru, had responded encouragingly as early as 1964. My ambition was to feature in his weekly column but he deflected all efforts towards his *London Evening News* slot. I liked his bluffness. He addressed me as 'Dear Groves', the handwritten *D* sometimes resembling a *P* and making me sound like orchards. Certain of my brain-teasing positions appeared in the newspaper on 5th July, 13th September, and 1st November 1965. Thereafter I submitted exclusively to *The Problemist*, a specialist periodical. A sunny letter to the Old Codgers graced the *Daily Mirror* of Friday 6th August 1965, sitting neatly above the comic strips Garth, The Larks, and The Flutters. Now that it is 1970, literary travail revolves around fashioning embryonic stanzas. Most never get beyond the longhand stage.

My father tends to the view that poets are unhinged. He wants me to open and close properly - in short, to be a good door - and presumes to have the only key. Thus he tells me on the afternoon of 19th July to wear my Sunday best. Are we going to church or meeting a business client? Mother drives us twenty-five miles to a zebra crossing outside Newport's Royal Gwent Hospital, scene of so much personal activity five years before. "Why have we stopped?" I ask uneasily, indignant at being kept in the dark. He climbs out, stretches, and walks to the far Belisha beacon where a shadowy female waits. She becomes mildly animated, shakes his hand, and smiles. What *is* this? She accompanies him to the car. He opens the door, the soul of courtesy, and she gets in, pleased to see me. I blush, flustered, and we motor off to a Berni Inn for drinks. Hell's teeth! It's a set-up.

"I hope you didn't mind me responding to your advertisement," Anthea Sutcliffe coos. The obvious reply is 'What advertisement?' I'm too embarrassed to answer, and shake my head vaguely. "Cheer up, it may never happen!" she twitters over a lager-and-lime. My conniving parents have positioned themselves at a far table so that we can become acquainted. It's excruciating. "I hear you write poems," she warbles. "What sort?" Oh, gawd! "My hero is William McGonagall," I lie. "Ever heard of him?" She also teaches, at some dilapidated primary school among the backstreets. Her father is a Brecon dentist and she has one sister. Her manner is mild; her eyes and hair are dark. She rents a flat at 43 Summerhill Avenue, Maindee, and says she finds it hard to get to know men. I sigh with an ancient world-weariness. Encouraged on all sides, I have little option other than to agree that she spend the next weekend at our home. Thus am I dragged, virtually kicking and screaming, into another relationship, feeling like a second-hand cooker or racing bike now that I've appeared in the Classified column of the *South Wales Argus*. What if she'd been a snaggletoothed booby? My father's gamble makes me annoyed and apprehensive.

In the fullness of time we have a few days away together. En route to Brighton we try kipping in the back of the Ford on the cold clear Sussex Downs. There's a tentative bit of how's-your-father which isn't much fun for either of us. She's as responsive as a lesbian. Given (a) our exertions, (b) the venue, and (c) the suspicion about her sexuality, I cannot help but think of American actor Dick Van Dyke. Soon I sense that instead of being unresponsive she is selectively thick-skinned; it would take a lot to make her cry though not much to make her angry. Beneath a placid exterior lurks a mercurial temperament. Add an adventurous streak and an offbeat sense of humour and you have quite a handful. The morning of Saturday 1st August is spent dozing on the resort's crowded beach, which I did with Roger Griffiths a couple of years earlier.

Emboldened by our preliminary jaunt, we resolve to go abroad together. The previous summer she'd met a Scandinavian teenager who had in a mad moment invited her to visit if ever she were near Hornslet, a town in Jutland, never imagining she would be taken up on it. So it is that we set off to thumb to Denmark, our knapsacks containing passports, a change of clothing, toiletries, and a road atlas of Europe. Our first night is spent at the Lansdowne Arms Hotel, Calne, where bed and breakfast costs £4 2s 6d. We take Room 19 and emphatically slough memories of that abortive business on the Sussex Downs. Next morning we continue our journey and eventually reach Dover where we check in at the youth hostel.

On Saturday 15th August we disembark at Zeebrugge after a four-hour crossing and hitch to Brussels. The following day we head for Rotterdam's 'De Windroos' hostel. Rain steadily falls. On the Monday we arrive in Amsterdam. One of the laid-back hippies loitering near the National Monument is freaking out. I ask a barefoot goddess with waist-length hair and a maxidress what's going on. "Oh, he's having a downer I guess. Lysergic acid. Thirty grams can give you two hundred thousand trips. Wanna try some?" Within the hour we are barrelling along the Ijsselmeer causeway. We stay successively at Sneek, Bremen, and Neumünster.

We enter Denmark at Kruså, rain dripping from our noses, cars flashing past with active wipers and small fountains of spray at each wheel, and get a lift the twenty-five kilometres to Åbenrå, where we stand fuming as the sun evaporates our dampness. A jolly woman calls across the road.

"English? Come, my darlings, let us speak." We shamble over to her Renault 4. She acts as if she's known us all our lives. "Ah! You must see Danmark - a very great country, yes?" Sensing we have nothing to lose and a fair amount of hospitality to gain, we nod enthusiastically. The three of us lurch forward and rattle off down the road to God-knows-where. Already she is singing nationalistic songs. She is around fifty and corpulent, with abundant curls and the manner of a Salvation Army major who's been at the sherry. We la-la to various anthems as the car threads along country lanes it seems to recognise. Without warning it turns into a field and we bump blithely over grass towards a mature copse. "Picnic, my dears!" Anthea and I exchange awe-struck glances. The old girl plainly couldn't give a toss about convention or common sense. Has she escaped from an asylum? The banger skids to a halt as she hauls up the handbrake, and we find ourselves beyond a wood beside a small cliff. Below us glistens the Baltic in general and Åbenrå Fjord in particular. Sure enough, she has food on board. "First we bathe!" She climbs out into a breeze which has set the trees gossiping, and descends to a shallow beach and ramshackle jetty. There is no sign of human habitation in any direction. Tall grass keels over, water rabbit-chops itself, and grey clouds roll in from an impatient sea. Already she is down to her bra and panties, and is still singing. She paddles furiously, as if she has a score to settle with the waves. Gritting my teeth, I doff my clothes. My partner does likewise. We tiptoe down cold hard sand and run into forbidding water. I force myself out further until my balls turn to concrete and the lower half of my body becomes numb. Anthea dips and prinks like a wading bird, seemingly unaware of the temperature. Our host is clearly in seventh heaven. Had film director Ingmar Bergman called 'Cut!' from some lofty vantage point I would not have welcomed a retake. Twenty minutes later we are huddled in her car, wrapped in blankets, spiritedly depleting a litre of Ålborg Akvavit. Although our flesh is slow to warm, in no time our stomachs are compact furnaces. The land miraculously loses its sharp edges; the brine begins to look less threatening. Three odd-balls voraciously rip apart a French loaf, gobble sild, and gorge chunks of Samsøe cheese.

Åbenrå is about the size of Port Glasgow though just a wee bit nicer. "You must have our proper Danish cuisine, not in the car, yes?" If you say so. We enter a spotless supermarket. Having been on the road for some days, we have begun subsisting on fruit and chocolate. The promise of home cooking concentrates the mind wonderfully. "You choose, guests!" Suddenly I am convinced of the existence of guardian angels. A total stranger is inviting us to empty the shelves. Through a haze of disbelief we hurry up and down aisles loading the trolley before the old bat changes her mind. Sumptuous fare accumulates: decadent pastries, expensive confectionery, pots of cream, sauces, steaks, wine. We call a halt in case our greed triggers an angry response, yet she pays without qualm and we sally forth to the parking lot. Almost immediately a thin middle-aged man approaches on a bicycle. He is surprised to see us but his wife waves him away with a single gesture. "Come, my dears. Let us get busy."

"Not so fast please," he says uncomfortably. "Where are you going?"

"Home," she trills. "See you soon." And off we speed to a neat suburban estate.

They live in a large modern house roofed with orange pantiles. Everything inside appears to be normal. Although my expression is neutral, I'm smiling madly. We put the cream in the capacious refrigerator, decant both bottles of Barolo, and leave the steaks, pastries, and candy on the work surface.

"What about your husband?" asks Anthea. "Will he mind us being here?"

"Let him, and see what happens," comes the mettlesome reply.

I decide to force the issue. "Look, it's getting late, and we won't be able to find a hostel if we have dinner with you."

The happy housewife beams at me. "No problem! We have a spare room." As my travelling companion and I have slept together only once, tonight looks set fair to be rounded off momentously. This really is too good to be true.

The long-suffering spouse lets himself in. There must have been a time when these two were enthralled by each other, and youth seemed never-ending and rich with promise. Their parrot shuffles and side-steps in its roomy cage, saying nothing and seeing everything, a tutelary spirit entrusted with ensuring they don't brain each other *just* yet. The husband tries out pleasantries with us but whenever he opens his mouth his wife squawks at him and he has to shut it.

The meal we Brits prepare, our hostess having locked herself in a bedroom to practise grand opera, is very good. She eventually joins us. The breadwinner is uncomplicated and clear-cut with a mild friendly manner. He proudly shows off some evening-class English:

> *Whether the weather is cold*
> *or whether the weather is hot*
> *we will weather the weather*
> *whatever the weather*
> *whether we like it or not.*

"Bravo," we cry, and the bird yawps from its perch. "Pah!" snorts the disgruntled diva, rising from the table. I am reminded of the Mad Hatter's Tea Party and expect our hostess to shout 'Off with his head!' at any moment. We wash up while a slanging match intensifies around us in a foreign tongue.

An hour later, while I try to read the Perletand toothpaste tube in the bathroom, all hell breaks loose with a theatricality which is as amusing as it is alarming. Anthea has already retired. As I turn off the light and step onto the landing the altercation rises momentarily in volume then falls correspondingly when I close the bedroom door behind me. George and Martha are tearing each other apart. Soon the curtain will fall and the audience applaud *Who's Afraid of Virginia Woolf*. Herr and Fru Pederson, or whoever they are, will stand centre stage and bow. There may be encores. While I am straddled in the scented darkness, the pandemonium reaches new heights. Crockery smashes, there's a psittacine screech, and inebriation combined with frustration, fear, and resentment produce a cacophony which counterpoints our bodies' rhythm. During a climactic hiatus everything falls eerily quiet... before the infernal engine starts up again. Disgust and tiredness eventually send the combatants to separate rooms and silence.

Tomorrow we shall pass within twelve kilometres of Egtved where a Bronze Age barrow has disclosed a young mother in an oak coffin. I toss and turn for hours under the duvet. Buried alongside are a child's charred remains. My dreams are primeval, troubled, inhabited by voices. The bog has uncannily preserved the woman, her clothing and ornaments, her ox-hide shroud and domestic utensils. She loosens her shackles and stalks the house, wailing for her lost infant. With a record of Carl Nielsen's opera *Maskarade* playing loudly, the lounge has become Copenhagen's Kongelige Teater. The bedside clock says 5:00. Thirty minutes later a large black car stops and a doctor and a male nurse stroll up the path. With the curtain pulled aside, we watch like children. Soon our hostess is led away and taken from our lives for ever.

We do not stay for breakfast. "Would you go," comes the exhausted plea. "Take food and leave." We do, thanking the husband for his kindness and saying it has been a night we will never forget.

To stand on the verge in the cool morning light with comfortable drivers, a surprising number in Opels, passing en route to work is a strange experience. Most know exactly where they are going. We do not. Will today yield another jolly eccentric or eight hours of joyless thumbing? Our destination is Denmark's second city, Århus. The map points us through towns we've never heard of. Cumulus cloud promises fair weather. Yesterday's events quieten us with their residual presence.

It takes longer than expected to reach our goal. Finally, near Skanderborg, we get a lift with four hippies. They say little (presumably understatement is cool) yet regard us immediately as kindred spirits. So long as there's free nourishment and accommodation at the end of the rainbow neither of us cares what colours it contains. It transpires that these flower children, two guys and two chicks who call themselves students, occupy a large upper-floor flat in a converted warehouse. It turns out to be surprisingly clean and tidy, though it does lack a bed, a carpet, a table, and a television. The magnificent floorboards, littered with scatter cushions, are used to eat and sleep on.

First we organise chow. Everyone helps. They understand English, after a fashion. Following a macrobiotic meal, joints are circulated. Next they settle down for a spot of meditation, so Anthea and I stroll around nearby streets for a while, buying postcards and trying the local Ceres beer as evening gently expires. When we return supper is ready. We sit cross-legged and tuck in and talk. The framed prints are international: Cartier-Bresson, Modigliani, some chinoiserie. The three-dimensional artefacts are comparably eclectic: bright wooden apples, a large fabric tiger, an ornate antique sword. Someone yawns. Someone else uses the bathroom. Tomorrow we will reach Hornslet and render a certain young woman speechless by our presence, but now it is bedtime. Futons are unrolled; duvets materialise; clothes are shed; a naked male puts the cat out; a female unselfconsciously discards her smock, revealing exquisite breasts, then pulls down her pants and drops them in the linen basket. I pretend not to notice. Suddenly it seems boringly British to be bothered by flesh and its revelation. Nobody tells us where to sleep. It appears we're to kip down together.

"Is there room for everyone?" I twitter.

The taller guy shrugs. "Maybe. I hope so."

I have a quick pee, keen not to be the prune on the end. If that can be avoided there's an even chance I'll be sleeping next to some Danish crumpet. There's no folderol with nightdresses and pyjamas. A bird's-eye view would distinguish us thus: Anthea, me, a blonde, a blond, a blonde, a blond. What next? Is there going to be a group grope? Probably not, though there could well be some subtle eroticism. Lights are switched off and silence reigns except for the sound of muted traffic and regular breathing. I place my right hand on a fairly familiar crotch. We lie like cathedral effigies. On my other side a voluptuous body turns and I feel the soft heaviness of breasts against my upper arm. I brush my left hand against her pubic hair. This raises no objection.

For the first and almost certainly the last time in my life I drift off to sleep stroking two pussies. Just for once whatever dreams arrive will be inferior to reality. Are these people shy, decorous, or shot through with Lutheran values? I shall never know. Suffice it to say that sexual abstinence is the order of the night. I am both disappointed and relieved. Orientals doubtless rise with a song in their hearts; a westerner unused to this type of bedding doesn't. I wake stiff in all the wrong places. The lush coppices I was touching last night have become buttocks, book ends to the single volume of my consciousness. Everyone else is asleep. It must be around 5.30. I stare at the ceiling until slumber returns.

Although Inge Glibstrup and her family live on a farm with thousands of pigs, during our stay I do not see one. Anthea and I telephone from Hornslet. Sure enough, our hostess-to-be is caught unawares yet has little option other than to affect delight at our arrival. She jumps into a truck and drives the short distance from the hamlet of Knagstrup to collect us. There are several bales of hay and a dog in the back. The sun shines and it's good to be alive. We are ushered indoors. No one else speaks English but everyone grins warmly.

A week in a traditional residence with local produce and lots of relaxation sounds ideal, especially when you aren't paying. Oh, before leaving we'll bestow a small gift to make good this glorious example of sponging off fellow Europeans in the name of international friendship. We ought to be ashamed of ourselves. Each of us has a room with solid old-fashioned furniture, a faded carpet, displays of dried grasses and seedheads, and rustic watercolours from our Victorian (their Christian IXth) era. Inge is twenty and charming, a bit spotty yet with a healthy body and bright eyes. Somewhere in the background a fiancé lurks. We get to meet him in due course. Mostly it's warm bread and fresh milk and free-range eggs and salubrious quietude at this her childhood home.

There must be a fly in the ointment. Things cannot stay so smooth. At lunch my presentiment objectifies with unnerving literalness. Flies. There are more than twenty in the dining room alone and they aren't in retirement. They're engaged in team games such as racing each other over the crackers, skating on the butter, hang-gliding from the milk jug. Not only that, one tries its hand at speleology by attempting to enter a nostril. I snort with disgust. My fellow diners look up.

Inge says, "Don't worry about them, Paul. It comes from living on a pigsty." I do not correct her malapropism. She adds, as if to reassure me further, "Generally they crawl over the animals, not over us."

Although the provender is grand, little of it passes my lips. Revenge is planned so that tea can be eaten carefreely. Once the meal is cleared, certain of these airborne invaders retire to the conservatory to bask in the sun. My incisors sharpen, my eyes redden, and I begin to growl. Brandishing my passport, I creep towards them. After a quarter of an hour there are thirty-eight corpses.

The days pass agreeably, thanks to the lovely weather:

great for photography had I bothered to bring a camera. We visit Rosenholm Castle, the delightful resort of Ebeltoft, and the chocolate-box houses of Århus Old Town. Eventually we say goodbye, promising to stay everlastingly in touch, and (having lied through our teeth) leave for Esbjerg, one-hundred-and-fifty kilometres away and nineteen hours from Harwich by DFDS ferry.

It's my first North Sea crossing. Our fares total 480 kroner. We share an airless four-berth cabin in the bowels of the ship. The low-pitched engine rhythm is that of a Palm Court orchestra reduced to one manic bassist who's never heard of sleep. The insistent thumping and the equally insistent swell and roll induce a sort of hypnotic hysteria which Anthea attempts to alleviate by dragging me off to a washroom and insisting we perform like Great Danes. The vessel continues its act of faith, generator rampant, shaft spinning, and screw mightily propelling our mass across unfathomable depths.

We avoid further hitchhiking and catch the train to Liverpool Street from Parkeston Quay. A few hours later we leave the Piccadilly Line at Finsbury Park and tramp towards Roger Griffiths's flat at 96 Wilberforce Road. As he's not at home, we pick the lock and move in for a couple of days.

Is this love? Certainly not. We would both acknowledge as much. It's little more than youthful opportunism, which isn't an indictable offence. What of the future? Being in your early twenties and unmarried can pose problems. The mating instinct impels you, and the question 'Would you like to spend the rest of your life with this person?' pecks at your brain. If the answer is 'No' the dilemma stays unresolved and another negative accumulates. The more you amass the more you need one positive to redress the balance.

We return to respective jobs. Although I spend weekends in glamorous Newport our relationship stagnates. She tells me her erratic mood changes (elation alternating with despair) are because she's manic-depressive. Having said that, the girl downstairs really is in a bad way. She had a baby by a Spaniard after a whirlwind romance and now lives surrounded by squalor. Surfaces are cluttered with grimy dishes, cat food, toys, eyebrow pencils, stockings, hairgrips, rolls of wallpaper, letters, records, nappies, newspapers.... No apology is made for the mess. Her inner disharmony is externalised and depersonalised. She doesn't sound the least bit dejected. To listen to her you'd think it was the flat that needed a psychiatrist. The toddler is also blithely untroubled and usually has a jammy face.

"Let's take her off for the day - get her out of herself," says Anthea. I agree and we plump for Cheddar Gorge. Buoyed up by a sparkling weather forecast, we pile into my van, head for the Severn Bridge, and reach the Mendips by early afternoon. The girl from the flat downstairs suggests we scale the side of the chasm. Anthea demurs. Three of us go ahead and eventually reach the top. There we recline, breathless and not a little hot and bothered. I chew on a blade of grass. The boy plays with a stick. His mother studies her split ends.

Half an hour later we start to descend as the sun is sinking and shadowing the valley. Just then we hear something between a shout and a scream. We'd left Anthea dozing in the van. Is she being attacked? We scuttle down the precipitous slope to the lay-by where we'd parked. The vehicle is empty. We call her name repeatedly but there's no reply. We drive up and down the road a few times. Nothing. We resolve to return to Newport and, if she still isn't to be found, contact the police. On arrival in Maindee we try the ground-floor door that gives access to her first-floor flat. It's bolted, rendering my key useless.

I shout through the letterbox: 'Anthea, are you in there? What the devil's going on?"

A chilling yell reverberates around the building. "Leave me alone. I hate both of you. Go away." We blink with disbelief. Has she flipped her lid? Has some doolally virus from

Åbenrå finally struck?

"Look - open this door."

"Go to hell!"

A muddy brick from the garden smashes the calm of the evening. My hand inches through the hole in the jagged glass and the latch is slid back. We rush upstairs and burst into her lounge. She isn't there or in the scullery. I enter her bedroom. The curtains are flapping. She's jumped out of the window! The single mum rushes to the lawn to administer first aid or last rites while I attempt to evaluate the situation and how I might explain things to neighbours, relatives, and the law. There's a further rumpus as someone runs downstairs. I peer out and discover no sheer drop but the tops of two bay windows. She's stepped onto one, leapt across onto the other, climbed into her living room, and vamoosed.

Although she doesn't admit it, her fit was triggered by insecurity. She feared her neighbour was about to steal her boyfriend. Thereafter we must pretend nothing untoward has happened. This is all very well until the next time and the time after that. As I'm getting blamed for her behaviour she must be taught a lesson. This entails an uncharacteristic level of deceit and an unpleasant sting. Just when she thinks she has me back on a string I arrange for us to see a film at the town's Dolman Theatre. Meanwhile I contact Joy, my old flame from the Forest of Dean. We haven't got together for ages yet she's still quite keen on me. Anthea and I are to rendezvous at 7.15 in the foyer. At 7.12 my former girlfriend visits the powder room. I vacantly sip a gin and tonic. Precisely on cue the victim shows. I smile and raise a hand... ... at someone from West Gloucestershire who struts towards me looking like a dog's dinner, takes my arm, and escorts me into the auditorium. The timing is superb and I feel exultant. It's not until much later that I regret my conduct.

After an eventful summer, work restarts at Lydney Boys' School. The atmosphere is considerably less rarefied than at St. Michael & All Angels. I mix with people who have blood rather than communion wine in their veins. You can relax each evening and not worry about the difference between consubstantiation and transubstantiation. Regular employment butters my bread and fills my fuel tank. Dud verse gets written, submitted to magazines, and rejected. Many of my pupils will hardly transcend dole queue or dead-end job; there's no way they're competing with, say, pupils at Winchester College. The fact that I'm not competing with masters at Winchester College has yet to register.

Before I encounter my wife-to-be, Cupid looses one more arrow, plucked from the quiver on Saturday 5th September 1970 as I head south along the A466 bound for an evening alone in Bristol. Two girls are thumbing near the village of Brockweir. I skid to a halt. They are eighteen years of age and have ebullient personalities. We reach romantic old Clifton as it lights up, agree on a meal, and enter a basement trattoria in Boyce's Avenue. After a high-spirited time, I bring them to Chepstow Youth Hostel. Thus begins the penultimate shot in the dark, the swan song of adolescence.

Philippa Gilbert, the more striking, has been close to a guy named Martin for three years. Although they now go divergent ways - he into banking, she into teaching - she says she's still in love with him. Nonetheless, she writes to me, I write to her, and she invites me to weekend at her Pinner home. Her widower father works for Air Traffic Control in West Drayton, and her brother Nick is at Brentwood School in Essex. They own a 1960 Ford Classic and a motorboat. She's an old girl of St Margaret's, Bushey, and a student at Wall Hall College, soon to become Hertfordshire College of Higher Education.

My memory is of a slim well-proportioned woman with strong teeth and lustrous hair who lists her vital statistics as 'too flat, too fat, and good enough for child-bearing'. She's majoring in Religious Studies and is much taken with German theologian Gerhard von Rad. I'd come across his writings at Llandaff but had never got round to tackling his *Die Theologie des Alten Testaments*. Much of the time she hides in books in order to get over the break-up with Martin. To this end she embraces any 'heavy' writer who promises spiritual uplift. She reads Hermann Hesse's *Demian* - appropriately an examination of self-awareness by a troubled teenager - and *Steppenwolf*; then *Lunar Caustic* by Malcolm Lowry, a writer who for ten years shared my 28th July birthday. Nothing helps. That said, her letters are balanced, mine are not. This is either because I'm tiring of trite romances or because I realise from the outset she's haunted by the past and I'm living too far away to enliven the present. I suspect she will settle for some staunch fellow student as soon as she can. Could it be a chap named Ian who is increasingly part of the furniture, or her 'Freudian friend' in Nottingham? I have an outside chance so apply for a post at nearby Woodhall School, South Oxhey. Despite my sound interview, the attempt is abortive.

Philippa catches the 14.45 from Paddington, arriving in Gloucester at 16.53 on Friday 23rd October 1970. After work I tear up from Lydney in my rustmobile to meet her. It's a lovely autumnal day. We meander back through Ross-on-Wye and Monmouth towards my rural home. Shadows lengthen and there's a nip in the air. We go for a few walks and she falls in love with the village and its wooded surroundings. Her stay is too brief and she must return to the din and distraction of the city. When I visit some time later I cannot get to grips with the situation. There's an invisible barrier. We are never alone together. Her sibling intrudes; or she must run an errand; or her parent, the urbane Henry, butts in. All I get is blithe, exasperating feyness: anthroposophy, eurythmy, Quakerism, Tolkien, yoga. We see *Downhill Racer* at the Essoldo, Chelsea - and, natch, Nick comes too.

What's to be done? I buy her dad a box of cotton handkerchiefs for his fifty-fifth birthday and woo his daughter with presumptuous verse:

> *Indian sandals streamlined in black*
> *Leather. Boots which peel like snake*

Skins. A coat with a round buckle.
You inside it, resolutely fickle,
Daring, an empress with high noble
Features, yet cursed with global

Doubts half-understood. You remain
Alarmingly beautiful, unsound in my brain.

Despite this she keeps in touch. "Take care of your mind," she says, 'it's very precious." That's reassuring - unless she's giving general advice in the area of mental health. She sends me screeds on stretches of shiny toilet paper; it saves on the Basildon Bond, I suppose. I send her various unenlightening snippets, and whinge and agonise introspectively page after page. She suggests: "Take twenty Seconal tablets with one large glass of whisky three times a day while sitting on a small thermonuclear bomb with a polythene bag over your head." I tell risqué jokes. She reads Dietrich Bonhoeffer's *Letters and Papers from Prison*. When next I appear on the scene I naïvely try to impress by wearing fancy gear purchased in Petticoat Lane. She is unimpressed. It's the ruse of the stickleback or bowerbird but they don't have to make advances from a distance of one-hundred-and-forty miles. Everything is uncertain. Most of my generation seem in a comparable state of flux. Jimi Hendrix chokes on his vomit. Janis Joplin croaks the next month from smack. Paul McCartney goes solo and temporarily hits the bottle. I hear a few tracks from his first LP in her Otterspool Hostel room. Again we aren't alone. Six others sit around sniffing joss sticks, nibbling nuts, sipping cider. She, regal and distant, holds court in the midst of this soiree. Nearby lurks the redoubtable Ian. It really is a dreadful yawn.

The bumf letters reach the end of the roll. What good have they done? She's eternally grateful for having been introduced by me to Colin Wilson's *The Outsider*. I'm pleased she has opened a door onto another vista, even if the wind of chance constantly threatens to slam it shut. We are never less than friends; the trouble is, we are never more than friends. The next I hear, she and Ian have a holiday job at a hotel in the Italian Alps. They marry on Saturday 27th May 1972 and settle in Handsworth, Birmingham. Her surname becomes Ward. The line goes dead. I am two dozen years old and feel like two thousand. The heavy neutral vastness of the universe doesn't mind one bit.

My grey matter has been primed by relationships that pass in the night, and I'm uneasy, bored, and charged with directionless emotion, feeling like Dylan Thomas before opening time. Although the literary production line slowly climbs the graph, progress is like hiking in the Cairngorms in low cloud. My father pooh-poohs my labour. He calls it 'airy-fairying' and fears for my sanity. Perhaps he has a point. Wordsworth said, in *Resolution and Independence* (1807),

> *'We poets in our youth begin in gladness*
> *But thereof comes in the end*
> *Despondency and madness.'*

Is it a coincidence that Byron, Coleridge, Dante Gabriel Rossetti, Goethe, and Shelley were manic-depressive, or that five Pulitzer-winning poets, among them Sylvia Plath, committed suicide? Dryden observed in *Absalom and Achitophel* :

> *'Great wits are sure to madness near alli'd*
> *And thin partitions do their bounds divide.'*

Despite this, I beaver away and am rewarded when D.J. Enright accepts 'Hummingbird' for *Encounter*. Five months later Alan Ross takes 'Clothed Man Ascending A Staircase' (loosely based on Marcel Duchamp's painting and X.J. Kennedy's poem) for *London Magazine*. It's the first time I've appeared in either journal. Otherwise there's a steady stream of rejection slips, which prompts me to seek professional assistance.

I apply to attend 'The Experience of Poetry', a Department of Education and Science course at York University from 4th-11th July 1972. Its leader is Seamus Heaney. Of the guest speakers, Thomas Blackburn turns out to be the most arresting. William Plomer, white-haired and gentlemanly, effortlessly commands respect. Edwin Brock is engagingly laconic. Seamus presides amiably. We spend time in my room talking about verse. He's approachable and unfazed by encroaching fame. I shudder when he's later burdened with Robert Lowell's tag: 'The best Irish poet since Yeats', a formidable weight to carry. He finds the sheaf of work I show him 'impressive' though he says I'm a bit sophisticated at present and need to become more elemental. To this end he lists titles to hang poems from, which include 'Burning Sticks', 'Epithalamion', 'Floods', 'Stillborn Child', and 'Swamps'. I'm keener on *vers de société*: Plomer's 'A Ticket for the Reading Room', say, or 'The Playboy of the Demi-World: 1938'. We form groups to discuss the likes of Anthony Hecht and Gerard Manley Hopkins. At the end of the week each of us presents a favourite poem. I choose Thomas Hardy's 'Timing Her' which goes down well. During the last-night party Vernon Scannell gets arseholed and has to be carried to his room.

Heaney must visit Gloucestershire for the christening of his niece Daisy Garnett. He's unsure of the route and asks if he can follow me. On Tuesday 11th July we hump suitcases into our cars, bid farewell to the others, and beetle off. For four hours his battered blue Volkswagen sits in my rear-view mirror. When we stop at the divergence of the M5 and M50 before going separate ways he invites me to send him a representative body of work. This he enthusiastically commends to Faber & Faber and it appears in *Poetry Introduction 3*. Craig Raine's submission for the same volume is turned down. Not for the first time I wonder at the way the spun coin falls. Soon Tom Paulin reads a selection of my verse at a National Book

League reception I'm unable to attend, and Douglas Dunn writes to request new material for an issue of *Poetry Review* he's editing. Robert Louis Stevenson was wrong: it is better to arrive than to travel hopefully.